BABA
The Devotees' Questions

Today, the Sai movement is a global phenomenon. The devotees want to have more and newer information about Sai Baba. During his travels across India and many countries of the world like USA, UK, Australia, Canada, and New Zealand for the inauguration of Shirdi Sai Baba temples and related activities, the author comes in touch with many devotees who ask a number of questions. Their genuine interest and inquisitiveness has propelled him to write this book, which is so vitally needed to answer their queries. The author answers the questions comprehensively, in a simple to understand manner.

The earlier book by the author, based on Questions and Answers, *Baba May I Answer*, had a tremendous response from the devotees, who found it very useful. This book, too, will definitely help the devotees to know more about their beloved Shirdi Sai Baba.

श्रीसांई सचरित

श्री:
साईनाथप्रभा.
SAINATHPRABHA
Kiran 1.
किरण १ ले.

साईनाथ-प्रभा ही प्रकाशित ह्वर्ची मावळी अंधकार । मायेच्या संभ्रमाचे छन-दळ उडे जें सदा हरितार ॥ श्रीसा विलसतसे किरण सगळे मकरंदसारी ॥ पाहोनि, चित्तकाशीं स्थिरदु जनमना संबंधा कांस्तरीं ॥

CONTENTS.
1. My Sai Baba—by Ram Gir.
2. Publisher's Note.
3. Approaches to Saipa bād—by Ram Gir.
4. Snakebite—by Ram Gir.
5. For visitors to pick up—by Ram Gir.
6. Shree Sai Nath and Shirdi by Sundarmo.
7. How unpleasant societies and their troubles developed—by Sundarao Narayan.
8. A Vision by Ram Gir.
9. Sai Nath Prabha Genis—by Ram Gir.

विषय.
१ वंदन-पंचक (कविता) हे० किरात.
२ 'साई' दरबारची महिमा (कविता) हे० सिं० हरिराम.
३ श्रीसाईनाथ व शिर्डी हे० किरात.
४ विराटस्वरूप श्रीसाईनाथ. (कविता) हे० पंडत रामलाल.

प्रकाशक:
दक्षिणाभिक्षा संस्था, हाईदराबाद-दर्क (हिंदी.)
[परिछ १९२६.]
किंमत ०-६-०

BABA
The Devotees' Questions

Dr. C. B. Satpathy

STERLING PAPERBACKS
An imprint of
Sterling Publishers (P) Ltd.
Regd. Office: A-59, Okhla Industrial Area, Phase-II,
New Delhi-110020. CIN: U22110PB1964PTC002569
Tel: 26387070, 26386209; Fax: 91-11-26383788
E-mail: mail@sterlingpublishers.com
www.sterlingpublishers.com

BABA: The Devotees' Questions
© 2014, Dr. C. B. Satpathy
ISBN 978 81 207 8966 1

All rights are reserved.
No part of this publication may be reproduced, stored in a retrieval system or transmitted, in any form or by any means, mechanical, photocopying, recording or otherwise, without prior written permission of the author.

Printed in India

Printed and Published by Sterling Publishers Pvt. Ltd., New Delhi-110020.

Preface

One of my books, written in English and titled *Baba May I Answer*, was published in 2009 by Sterling Publishers, Delhi, and has since been reprinted a few times. This book has also been translated in various national languages like Hindi, Odia, Assamese, Tamil, Telugu, Punjabi, Marathi, Gujarati, and Bengali. It has been translated in Nepalese as well. The publishers inform me that this book and its translated versions, particularly in English, are in great demand.

When I visit countries like the USA, UK, Australia, Canada, and New Zealand for the inauguration of Shirdi Sai Baba temples and related activities, I come in touch with a large number of devotees of Baba who ask a number of questions. Their genuine interest and inquisitiveness has propelled me to write this book, which is so vitally needed to answer their queries.

I have been writing on various aspects relating to Shirdi Sai Baba and have been imparting discourses to Sai devotees in India and abroad for the last two decades. My articles have been published in magazines like *Sai Bani, Sai Darpan, Sai Chhaya* in Odia; *Heritage of Shirdi Sai, Sai Vichaar* (e-magazine) in English; *Sai Kripa, Sai Baba Darshan, Sai Charan, Sai Lehar, Sai Raksha* in Hindi; *Sai Ananta* in Marathi; *Sai Kirnalu* in Telugu; and also in some bilingual magazines like *Sai Arpan* and *Sai Prabha* (in Hindi and English). The material contained in this book in the Question and Answer form is not a reproduction of my speeches and writings. I have tried to answer the queries, asked to me by many devotees from India and abroad, in a comprehensive manner.

This book may not be taken as an updated version of the previous book because a majority of the questions and answers are new. This book also has some special features which the earlier book, *Baba May I Answer*, does not contain.

My Questions and Answers pertaining to (a) The bilingual (English and Marathi) magazine *Sainath Prabha*, which used to be published in Shirdi between the years 1916 and 1919, (b) Information contained in the intelligence report of the British Government (CID) on Baba, and (c) The school in which Shama worked as a teacher and which has been demolished, may be of great interest to the devotees. I have specially incorporated a chapter for the benefit of international devotees, who I meet often in the US and other countries. Today, the Sai movement is a global phenomenon. The devotees want to have more and newer information. I hope that this book will help them to know more about Baba.

I take this opportunity to convey my appreciation to Ms Shipra Shukla for collecting, collating, and correcting the different articles and question and answers published in various magazines. She has also been collecting relevant anecdotes from Shri Sai Satcharita and related books. My personal gratitude goes to Mr Snehasish Ray and Ms Neha Sikka for correcting and assembling the manuscript assiduously and earnestly over a period of several months. These earnest Sai devotees have helped me a lot in the completion of this book. May Shri Sai bless them all to continue to work for His cause in future.

I thank Mr Mukund Raj of Chicago for helping me to complete the question and answers of the section which is meant for international devotees. Last, but not the least, I thank Mr S. K. Ghai, Managing Director, Sterling Publishers Pvt. Ltd., for undertaking the publication of this book. May Shri Sai bless them all.

C. B. Satpathy
cbs432@gmail.com

Contents

	Preface	v
1.	The Sai Movement	1
2.	Temples	3
3.	Worship and Prayers	5
4.	Faith and Devotion	13
5.	Suffering of the Devotees	19
6.	Dreams	29
7.	Yoga	31
8.	God, Religion, Path, and Philosophy	33
9.	The Master and the Disciples	62
10.	Shirdi Sai Baba and Sadgurus (Perfect Masters)	75
11.	Spiritual Education	126
12.	Experiences	129
13.	Questions from International Devotees	138

1

The Sai Movement

Q. How can one join the Sai movement?

A. Any devotee of Shri Sai or any person with an honest intention to serve the Sadguru can join the Sai movement. Such a person should have faith in Him and should be willing to work for the ideals for which Baba stood. We should never compare ourselves with others thinking that we are too great or too insignificant to work for the Master. If a person reads Shri Sai Satcharita, he will find that many types of people from different rungs of society, high and low, used to work for Baba, for example, Kaka Saheb Dixit, the famous solicitor from Mumbai; Nana Saheb Chandorkar, the Magistrate; Das Ganu, the Police Constable; and Shama, the teacher at the lower primary school at Shirdi.

Baba was aware of the capabilities of all His devotees. Each of them performed certain functions that were allocated to them by Baba, in accordance with their abilities. Due to the ceaseless efforts of these devotees, the Sai movement went beyond the boundaries of Shirdi village to different parts of India. Presently, the Sai movement has become a global phenomenon.

Any devotee residing at any place in the world can join this movement and contribute in accordance with his capacity. With the increasing use of internet, it is easier for the devotees to communicate with one another and take the Sai movement forward. This was not possible thirty years ago.

Different organizations propagating the name of Baba have come up in different countries in the world. They have built several temples and, besides conducting the worship of Baba, are carrying out social service projects for the local communities as well. Those interested can join with one another and expand the global Sai movement. The time has come for the Sai devotees to do whatever they have been wishing to do since long for the cause of Baba.

2

Temples

Q. What is the main purpose of building temples of Baba?

A. Human beings belonging to different religions and living in different parts of the world have been building places of worship called by different names such as temple, church, mosque, pagoda, Govind Wada, etc. A temple is supposed to be a building for religious congregation and used by the devotees for performing religious rites, prayers, and preachings. The religious places also try to give shelter to the destitute, food to the poor, and medical aid to the sick and the poor. These are the traditional practices followed by the temples.

A temple is the home of the deity and people visiting it should be treated with respect. There should be no discrimination between human beings in a temple because they are all the children of God. Baba stayed most of His life in a dilapidated masjid called Dwarkamayi, but He never called it His temple. For Him, it was His home and also the home of His devotees. There, He used to treat the sick, feed the hungry, teach the ignorant, encourage music and the study of scriptures, and performed many other activities for social good. Therefore, the temples built in His name, where His statue is installed, should be used for such purposes. The performance of daily pujas and celebration of religious functions alone is not enough.

Q. Which religious festivals should be celebrated in Sai temples?

A. A number of religious festivals can be celebrated in the temples of Shri Shirdi Sai Baba following the tradition of Baba's temple at Shirdi. The most important functions are Ram Navami, Dussehra and Guru Poornima. Shri Dattatreya Jayanti, Maha Shivratri, Shri Krishna Janmashtami are also celebrated in most of the temples dedicated to Baba. Every year, we can also celebrate the foundation day of the temple or the day on which Baba's statue was installed in the temple as well.

Q. Why don't people come to the Sai temple with a sense of real devotion? I feel sad about it.

A. This is a presumptuous view. When a person thinks that he alone knows what devotion means and not others who visit the temple, he is becoming self-opinionated. However, it is a different question if one takes the decent comportment of others as an indicator of real devotion. Further, except Baba, who else is the receiver of the devotion? Who else can understand the depth of devotion of a devotee? It is better not to entertain such thoughts in mind. We should not suffer from a sense of spiritual superiority and judge the devotional levels of others from our limited perspective.

3

Worship and Prayers

Q. **Many people speak of "Manasa Puja". What is Manasa Puja and how is it performed?**

A. Manasa Puja or mental puja is a process in which the worshipper goes through a mental process the entire ceremony of a certain puja that he usually performs when sitting in front of a statue or a picture of a Deity or Guru. For example, when we perform any puja, normally we try to concentrate on the statue or the picture of the Deity, offer naivedya, and perform aarti. We complete the entire process of puja, stage by stage. We use many items for the puja. In Manasa Puja, the detailed acts of the puja are performed mentally, visualizing the same process and stages. Keeping his eyes closed, the devotee focuses his inner mind on the image of the Deity or Guru. He goes on to perform each stage of puja like bathing, clothing, decorating the statue, offering naivedya, and performing aarti in front of the mental image of the Deity or Guru, in his mind, as if it were real. While doing so, the worshipper does not cut short on the time of the actual puja. Material puja items are not needed for conducting such a puja.

Initially, it is difficult to perform Manasa Puja, but after a lot of practice, the performance of the Manasa Puja becomes easy. The benefit of such a system of puja is that it can be performed at any place and at any time, even in the absence of material items required for a puja. However, it is advisable to perform the mental puja at a fixed time and for a fixed period of time when you are at home or away from home. It is more difficult to perform Manasa Puja than the normal puja that people generally follow. It is advisable to perform actual puja in the first stage and Manasa Puja in the second stage.

Q. Can ritualistic worship be called spirituality?
A. Yes and no. Based on their level of consciousness, devotees follow different methods and traditions in the performance of puja. One devotee may offer gold, money, fruits, etc., to God or Guru, whereas a poor devotee may offer a tulsi leaf, fruits, or rice grains, etc. Shri Krishna has expounded the theory in the Gita that if the devotion is pure and intense, even the simplest of offerings is accepted by God.

Offering costly material things to God, when lacking in *bhava*, is a futile exercise. Baba has said that internal worship or prayer with bhava is the best form of worship. In other words, if a devotee has pure bhava, single pointed concentration, and pure consciousness, then regardless of how he worships, it is accepted by God.

Some devotees worship the Lord from the innermost recess of their heart, instead of offering material objects to Him. Actually, this is the real path to spirituality. If God is worshipped only with the wish of fulfilment of worldly desires, then it is not spirituality. This is known as *sakama* form of worship (that is, performance of worship with self-interest) whereas God loves *nishkama* form of bhakti. How many of us are ready to accept whatsoever happens in our life — good or bad — and yet continue to love God and to worship Him? How many have become worthy of receiving the grace of God because of their kindness towards others? Instead of being self-centred, can we think of sacrificing a little for others? Unless we are able to awaken within us the conviction to render selfless service to others, we are not following the true spiritual path that Baba has prescribed.

Q. What is the meaning and importance of symbol worship or "Prateek Puja"?

A. Parabrahma or God has been visualized as an all-pervading and eternal reality by the saints and realized souls. They have also experienced the subtle and divine power of God. Devotees who have, with the grace of the Sadguru, experienced the Chaitanaya Roop (God as Pure Consciousness) of God may not perform worship of a symbol of God. They can worship God as an All-Pervading Consciousness. However, symbolic worship of statues, photos, pictures, etc., is required to be performed by the devotees who are at an early stage of their spiritual journey. Those who have not acquired the ability to link their consciousness with the all-pervading universal consciousness of God (by undergoing hard spiritual penance or yoga sadhana), find it easy to worship God in the form of a symbol. Through worship of the symbolic form of God, it is possible to graduate to the worship of the *nirakar* or formless aspect of God.

We worship God in the form of a statue because it is not so easy to mentally conceive the idea or image of the formless all-pervading God in our mind, which suffers from many limitations. Therefore, most of the spiritual practitioners worship the embodied form of God at the beginning. After succeeding in that, they start worshipping God without a form. Many saints worship the formless God. It can be said that Nirvikalp Samadhi is nothing but the experience of the formless God, who transcends all qualities, characteristics, attributes, and forms that exists in the universe.

> **Form and Formless Worship of Baba**
>
> Therefore, Baba said, "Meditate always on My formless nature, which is knowledge incarnate, consciousness, and bliss. If you cannot do this, meditate on My Form from top to toe as you see here, night and day. As you go on doing this, your *vrittis* will concentrate on one point and the distinction between the Dhyata (meditator), Dhyana (act of meditation), and Dhyeya (this meditated upon) will be lost and the meditator will be one with the Consciousness and be merged in the Brahman."
> (Chapters 18 and 19, *Shri Sai Satcharita*)

Q. **Can the worship of Sadguru be called Saguna Sakar form of worship?**

A. The Sadguru is an Embodied Divine Consciousness. Actually, the devotees initially worship the physical form of Sadguru. The word *sakar* in Hindi means "with a form" and *saguna* means "with divine attributes".

Q. **Sadguru is Saguna Sakar and the statues worshipped in the temple are also Saguna Sakar. What is the difference between the two and what are the different methods to worship them?**

A. The difference between a statue and Sadguru is that statues are made of inert objects like of stones, metal, or some other material whereas the Sadguru is a living form with the highest spiritual attribute, that is, Divine Consciousness. That is why during *prana prathistha* or installation of the statue, the priest recites the prana mantra to infuse the statue with prana, divine powers, and attributes. Further, when thousands of devotees go and focus their spiritual thoughts on the statue, it is believed to get surcharged with divine thought waves emanating from such thoughts and prayers. It is believed that the deities need to be propitiated through puja in order to get a boon. However, the devotees of a Sadguru can get blessings from a Sadguru even without performing such a puja.

The Sadguru who has realized God can be communicated with directly by the devotee, which we cannot do with a statue. Shirdi Sai Baba encouraged His devotees to continue with the worship of their personal deities as well. However, these devotees used to worship Baba, even while worshipping other deities of the Hindu pantheon. Baba used to encourage the devotees to continue to worship their personal or family deities.

> **Megha**
>
> Then Megha began to look upon Sai Baba as an incarnation of Shiva. In order to worship Shiva, *bael* leaves are required and Megha used to go miles and miles every day to bring them and worship his Shiva (Baba). His practice was to worship all the gods in the village and then come to the Masjid and after saluting Baba's gaddi (aasan), he worshipped Baba and after doing some service (shampooing His legs), drank the washings (Tirth) of Baba's feet. Once it so happened that he came to the Masjid without worshipping God Khandoba, as the door of the temple was closed. Baba did not accept his worship and sent him again, saying that the door was open then. Megha went, found the door open, worshipped the Deity, and then returned to Baba as usual. (Chapter 28, *Shri Sai Satcharita*)

Nevertheless, the fact remains that Shirdi Sai Baba, or for that matter other Sadgurus like Shri Ramakrishna Paramahamsa, Shri Akkalkotkar Maharaj, Samarth Ramadas, etc., guided, protected, and evolved their devotees directly.

Q. Is the worship of a photograph or statue of the Guru in accordance with the religious prescriptions of the Hindus?

A. Yes. Hinduism prescribes the worship of various deities, built by use of any of the eight materials, in creating the form of the deities in the Hindu Pantheon. The statues can be built of stone, metal, wood, leaf, sand, etc. A similar practice can be followed for the worship of the Sadgurus. The deities and Sadgurus can even be worshipped in the form of paintings and, in modern times, in the form of photographs. The fact is that in order to meditate on the form, there must be a symbol available to a devotee.

Q. Sometimes devotees feel bad when they are not able to follow the correct rites or rituals when performing a puja because they don't know the method. What should they do?

A. Different methods of worship have been prescribed for different deities in Hinduism. The rituals prescribe the different types of mantras and prayers and the use of different material for the purpose. There is a laid down procedure which has to be followed for each deity. The priests, who are trained in the methods of worship, are well equipped to perform the pujas. However, an ordinary person neither knows the mantras nor the procedure required for a particular puja. If a person is so desirous of conducting a puja but doesn't have the knowledge to do so, he can deploy a trained priest to do the job for him. He can also pick up books on Puja Vidhi, written in all the Indian languages, that are available in the market. A person can learn the basic methods of worship from these books. In that case, he will not suffer from the feeling of guilt that he is not able to perform puja properly at home. He can also get the puja done at any temple which undertakes to perform such activities.

Worship and Prayers

At home, a person can perform puja to the extent it is possible to do so—cleaning the statue, clothing it, decorating with chandan and vermillion tikka, garlanding it, lighting a lamp and incense sticks, and offering prasad. In case of worship of Shri Shirdi Sai Baba at home, devotees generally perform the puja in the manner stated above, in addition to singing Sai Aarti and reciting the prescribed mantras.

For the worship of Sai Baba, the material aspect of the puja is not as important as the devotional fervour with which the puja is conducted. It is the intense bhava of the devotee that attracts the Sadguru.

Q. It has been mentioned in Shri Sai Satcharita that some devotees used to recite Gayatri mantra before Baba in Dwarkamayi Masjid. What is the importance of this mantra and how should it be recited?

A. Gayatri is one of the most important and potent mantras of Hindu religion. The mantra is an invocation of the Sun God for granting divine knowledge, power, and devotion to the *sadhaka*. Gayatri is both a mantra and a prayer. Sun worship has been an ancient tradition, followed by various ancient religions, including Hinduism. The mantra is written in a poetic meter known as Anushthup and consists of twenty four syllables, which are divided into three groups, each consisting of eight words. It is said to have been composed by an ancient Rishi by the name of Shri Vishwamitra. In almost all the pujas and religious festivities of the Hindus, this mantra is required to be recited.

Gayatri Mantra Sadhana is one of the prescribed spiritual practices in Hinduism. It is usually recited early in the morning and at the time of sunset. Generally, the practitioners recite the mantras 108 times continuously or in a multiple of 108. In my view, this mantra can be recited, even mentally, without loud recitation. We can recite it whenever possible, without bothering for the number of chantings. A person who wants to perform Gayatri Sadhana can take deeksha from the Guru if the Guru so desires.

Q. Can Gayatri Mantra be recited at night?

A. Gayatri Mantra is usually recited in the morning and evening, that is, at the time of sunrise and sunset. It can be recited at any time of the day. But it should not be done at night because it is a mantra for the worship of the Sun God. It is understood that Gayatri Mantra in Tantra Sadhana is used at night.

4

Faith and Devotion

Q. How can we get rid of fear, apprehension, disbelief, etc., that grips our mind and does not allow us to be close to Sai Baba?

A. It is not correct to say that bad thoughts, fears, or apprehension in our mind do not allow us to come closer to Sadguru Shri Sai Baba. We should try to establish inner links with Baba even if these bad thoughts, fears, apprehension, or disbeliefs exist in us. Baba Himself has said that the devotees should "offer all the worries to Me and I will take care". Why not believe that Baba controls everything — good and bad — in the life of His devotees?

When fear, apprehension, or disbelief are generated within us, it provides us with an opportunity to overcome them and walk along the path of evolution. A problem may be defined as a situation waiting for a solution. Without the fear of God and spiritual support of the Guru, human beings would commit so many sins that they would not be able to survive. Without facing apprehensions, we cannot discipline our minds and streamline our lives. Without disbelief at the initial stage, belief or faith cannot become strong.

We can recollect the story of Swami Vivekananda who, at the earlier stages of his contact with Shri

Ramakrishna Paramahamsa, had a lot of disbelief about Him. However, with experience, he learnt that the Paramahamsa was a true saint. Shri Vivekananda is one of the rarest spiritual personalities who tested his Guru more than the Guru tested him, to be convinced about His divinity.

We must understand that the exercise to get rid of bad traits under the tutelage of the Sadguru will help us to attain virtues in the future. We should think that, for our evolution, Baba gives us all sorts of experiences. At times, when a devotee used to approach Baba to get divine help in order to solve his problem, Baba would give a certain command that would be extremely confusing to understand or hard to follow. However, if the devotee followed the command by going through all the trials and tribulations that it entailed, then he used to be benefited.

Sadasiva Tarkhad

Baba's care and help were also extended to her husband. For some time, he was the manager of a mill. Then his services were terminated and he had to remain for a considerable time without any job. He went to Shirdi in the hope that Baba would help him get a job. But soon after he reached Shirdi, Baba, instead of providing him with a job, told him, "Tatya Patil and others are going to attend a cinema at Ahmednagar. You better go with them and thence go home to Pune." He felt mortified that, without getting a job, he was asked to attend amusements.

Anyhow, Baba's order had to be obeyed. He went and attended the cinema and after leaving Ahmednagar, he went to Pune. But what a surprise! Baba, he had thought, had sent him to Pune simply for nothing. But at Pune, at the mill, a labour strike had broken out. The authorities

> concerned were anxious to recall him as he was a very capable manager of labour, and they had wired for him to Mumbai and other places. Meanwhile Baba, knowing of the wire and the situation, had sent him just in time to get his job. So Baba, appearing to be doing harm, really was conferring a blessing by His seemingly unkind orders. (Chapter 4, Part III, *Life of Sai Baba*, p. 524)

Q. How can we keep the light of faith burning within us?

A. The light of faith always burns in the soul of a true devotee, but in the case of most of human beings, it is covered with a few layers of coverings called "maya" or divine illusion. The question is, how can we remove the veil that covers the light of faith? For this, we have to have full faith in the Guru and follow His advice. If a devotee has surrendered to the Guru, he will always think about the Guru only and gradually he will experience His greatness, universality, and grace in anything and everything around him.

With such an experience, slowly but surely, the curtain of illusion or maya will vanish and the light of faith will shine brightly. Constant reading of books written on the lives of the Masters and the company of noble-hearted people will go a long way in keeping the light of faith burning in the soul. We can read Shri Sai Satcharita, through which we will come to know about the lives of Kaka Saheb Dixit, Tatya Kote Patil, Shama, Mhalsapati, and others, who used to be with Shri Shirdi Sai Baba. Faith or shraddha can only be sustained with the help of saburi or patience, as Baba used to say.

Q. What is the difference between bhakti in the traditional sense of the term and *raga-anuraga* bhakti?

A. A majority of the devotees generally follow a simple form of devotion. In religion, devotion means love for

God or Guru. Everybody loves God in some form or the other, displaying different types of spiritual emotions known as *bhava*. We can find the description of *navadha bhakti* (nine types of devotion) in Shri Sai Satcharita. There are several forms and levels of bhakti. Each devotee practices bhakti according to his *samskara* and the level of faith he has in the Guru. *Raga-anuraga* bhakti is the highest state of divine love. Such kind of intense divine emotions were exhibited by the gopis for Lord Krishna. Shri Chaitanya Mahaprabhu was instrumental in spreading *raga-anuraga* bhakti in the eastern part of India.

When a devotee emotionally connects with God or Guru in this manner, he becomes highly engrossed and becomes one with the Lord. Eight kinds of spiritual emotions manifest in him, for example tears flowing from the eyes, horripilation or hair standing up, shocks jolting the body, speechlessness, dancing in ecstasy, etc. In such a state of spiritual ecstasy, the devotee seeks only the God or the Guru and nothing else in the universe. He becomes oblivious of the world around, including his family and the society. All that matters to him is God or Guru; the rest of the world becomes meaningless to him. Intense love, at times, creates physical convulsions or change in the colour of skin (yellowish tinge). Sometimes even drops of blood ooze out from the pores of his skin and the corners of his eyes. He remains in a state of divine bewilderment or stupor for long hours. Unlike the other devotees, he does not even know how to glorify his Guru (as language fails him), but he loves Him intensely from the depth of his heart. He does not seek for liberation or emancipation. The deep love for God gives him a sense of fulfilment in life.

This intense devotional state is termed as *jalali* by the Sufi saints. Shri Sai Baba, Swami Ramakrishna

Paramahamsa, and Shri Chaitanya Mahaprabhu frequently used to enter into a *jalali* state. In a way, this *jalali* state of the Sufis may be termed as *raga-anuraga* bhakti. The only difference is that, whereas in the Shri Krishna cult Lord Krishna is taken as the only man and all others are women on earth, in Sufism God is taken as the beloved (in feminine form) and the Sufi saints as love-lorn devotees or lovers.

Q. What are the nine forms of bhakti and eight types of bhava as described in Hinduism?

A. The nine forms or types of bhakti, as defined in Hinduism, are (1) *Shravana* (Hearing); (2) Kirtana (Praying); (3) *Smarana* (Remembering); (4) *Padasevana* (serving the feet); (5) *Archana* (Worship); (6) Namaskara (respectful bow); (7) *Dasya* (divine servitude); (8) *Sakhyatva* (Friendship); (9) *Atmanivedana* (surrender of the self). Shirdi Sai Baba used to tell His devotees that if any of these is faithfully followed, Lord Hari will be pleased and manifest Himself in the home of the devotee.

A high level of spiritual ecstasy leads to motionlessness, perspiration, horripilation, indistinctness of speech, tremor, paleness, tears, and, at times, loss of consciousness.

The *Ashta Bhava* (eight bhava) are:
- Gurgling in the throat when speaking
- Horripilation, hair standing on end
- Dancing
- Shouting
- Indifference to other's views
- Falling or rolling on the ground
- Trance
- Speechlessness

The Eight *Satwik Bhava* (spiritual emotions of the devotee)

(233 and 234)
Eight types of devotional feelings (emotions) awaken and he gets drawn towards mental worship. By the grace (power) of Sadguru, the devotee receives divine knowledge. In a moment, the devotee remains blissful and in another moment, he behaves like a crazy person. At one moment, he is happy and in the next moment, he is depressed.

(235 and 236)
He sheds tears in the remembrance of the Guru and weeps without any reason. Immersed in the remembrance of the Guru, he is not attentive to himself (does not care about himself). He usually remains silent. He talks to his self. He always remembers his Guru in sleep, dream, and wakefulness.

(237 and 238)
Sporting a beard and unkempt hair, he roams around with a dispassionate mind. Without food and water, he looks like a mental wreck. Absorbed in "Guru-Prem", he wanders from place to place. Even though he looks restless from outside, (yet) his heart is at rest.

(239 and 240)
He partakes the leftover food of the Guru with love and eats with relish. The devotee is ever anxious to render services to the Guru. He does not like the world (worldly ways). Without the Guru, everything seems meaningless to him. His mind is ever anxious in the remembrance of the Guru.

(Vol. 1, *Shri Guru Bhagavat*, English translation by Shri Chandra Bhanu Satpathy, pp. 144–146)

5

Suffering of the Devotees

Q. **Why are the devotees of Baba so much in pain? Why do they suffer despite being Baba's devotees?**

A. On this earth, whether one is a devotee of God or a Guru, all are bound to go through some amount of suffering. The devotees do not necessarily suffer because they are devotees of Baba. They suffer due to the karma *prarabdha* of their past lives and of the present life as well. However, due to the kindness of Baba, their sufferings get reduced and the power of tolerance grows in them. Baba used to take care of all the devotees who came in His shelter.

All the devotees of Baba are certainly not in pain and never in pain always. A real devotee of Baba will not treat such worldly distresses as spiritual pain. The real pain for him will be the pain of separation from the Sadguru, even temporarily. It is the spiritual pain that brings the devotee closer to the Master. Even when undergoing mental or physical pain, he will be in a state of spiritual ecstasy, realizing the compassion and protection given by the Master. Usually, people afflicted by worldly needs and troubles come to Baba. There were a small number of devotees who used to come to Baba out of sheer love for Him without any material expectations.

Neither the spiritual nor religious scriptures, nor the Saints say that human beings will not suffer the worldly, mental, or physical problems because no one can go beyond the laws of nature.

Q. **Will Baba not listen to my prayers if I have committed some sins?**
A. The prayers of all, sinners and saints alike, are listened to by the Sadgurus and Saints, giving equal importance to all. The Sadguru does not hate a sinner. On the other hand, He tries to render as much help as possible, being aware that a sick or weak child needs more help. Continue to pray Baba to bestow His kindness on you. There can be no sin, howsoever evil, in this world which can go beyond the compassion of God. Continue to pray to Baba to remove the sinful proclivities from your mind and make your life peaceful and pure. Some of the natives of Shirdi who were charged with the offence of murder and were tried in the court of law were ardent devotees of Baba. Under the divine influence of Baba, their lives slowly changed.

Q. **I have done many things to keep others happy, but I got nothing except pain and sorrow in return. Why does this happen?**
A. By doing good to others, you not only exhaust your stock of sins carried forward from the past lives, but also accumulate a stock of virtue (*punya*). You will also develop the qualities of forgiveness and patience within yourself. Giving happiness to others brings you nearer to Baba. Baba Himself has said this.

> **Baba's Advice Regarding Our Behaviour**
>
> Shri Hari (God) will certainly be pleased if you offer water to the thirsty, bread to the hungry, clothes to the naked, and your verandah to strangers for sitting and

> resting. If anybody asks for money, you may not part with your money, but do not shout at him like a dog. Let anybody speak hundreds of things against you, do not react with bitter replies. If you always tolerate such things, you will certainly be happy. Let the world go topsy-turvy, you remain where you are. Standing or staying in your own place, calmly observe the show of things passing before you. (Chapter 18 and 19, *Shri Sai Satcharita*)

Giving happiness to others does not mean that a person will never get pain from those he has helped. Sometimes, the parents receive the maximum pain from their children, for whom they do so much. Every person cannot be expected to respond to kindness in the same manner.

A person should never expect goodness from others as a return for the goodness he has done to them, as it may lead to pain and disappointment when such expectations are not fulfilled. Your expectations should only be focused on spiritual personalities like Baba, because you will certainly receive His grace when you will need it the most. Keep on praying to Baba to sustain you on the correct path and grow patience in yourself to tolerate the imperfections of others. The stock of the good deeds of your past is there to help you in the future. Never give up the noble attitude of helping others simply because others don't appreciate or reciprocate it. At times, it takes a longer period of time for people to realize the virtue in others.

Q. For the last two months I am getting suicidal thoughts. How do I get rid of them?

A. You are a devotee of Shri Shirdi Sai Baba. If you have read Shri Sai Satcharita, you will come across the story of a devotee named Gopal Narayan Ambadekar of

Pune, who wanted to commit suicide as he could not deal with the misfortunes of life and how he was saved by the grace of Baba.

Shri Sai advises His devotees never to think of committing suicide. The *prarabdha* karma of a person does not get exhausted even if a person commits suicide. He has to face his karmic destiny in future lives, even if he wants to escape it through the route of suicide in this life. Getting rid of the present life and present relationships does not mean that we will be able to get rid of our *rina* or debt of the past lives. The act of suicide will create a huge *prarabdha* and will ruin the next life as well. It is better to keep unshakeable faith in the words of Baba and go through the difficulties in this life with equanimity.

God has placed you in much better circumstances in life compared to many other people who don't even have the basic minimum required to survive in life. You know the principles of business. You must know that we take birth in order to enable the soul to add to the value of its assets through spiritual evolution.

Gopal Narayan Ambadekar

Gopal Narayan Ambadekar of Pune was a devotee of Baba. He served for ten years in the Abkari department and retired. He tried to get some other job, but he did not succeed. He was overtaken by other calamities and his condition grew from bad to worse. He passed seven years in this condition, visiting Shirdi every year and placing his grievances before Baba. In 1916, his plight became worse and he decided to commit suicide in Shirdi. So he came there with his wife and stayed for two months. One night, while sitting in a bullock cart in front of Dixit Wada, he resolved to end his life by throwing himself into a well close by. He proposed to do this, but Baba

> wished something else. A few paces from this place, there was a hotel and its proprietor, Sagun, a devotee of Baba, came out and accosted him saying, "Did you ever read this Akkalkotkar Maharaj's life?" Ambadekar took the book from Sagun and began to read it. Accidentally, or we may say providentially, he came across a story which was to this effect: During the lifetime of Akkalkotkar Maharaj, a certain devotee suffered very much from an incurable disease and when he could endure the agony and pain no longer, he became desperate and to end his miseries, threw himself one night into a well. Immediately, the Maharaj came there and took him out with his own hands and advised him thus, "You must enjoy the fruit — good or bad — of your past actions; if the enjoyment is incomplete, suicide won't help you. You have to take another birth and suffer again; so instead of killing yourself, why not suffer for some time and finish up your store of the fruit of your past deeds and be done with it once and for all?"
>
> Reading this appropriate and timely story, Ambadekar was much surprised and moved. Had he not got Baba's hint through the story, he would have been no more.
> (Chapter 26, *Shri Sai Satcharita*)

Q. **Even when possessing a lot of power and wealth, some people feel dissatisfied and miserable? Why is this so?**

A. If a person has everything to his satisfaction, then, why would he feel miserable? There does not exist a single individual on this earth who possesses everything that he wishes for. Due to their limited intellect, human beings sometimes give more value to useless and nonessential things of life than what these things deserve.

Unfulfilled desires lead to suffering and frustration. Such desires can be material, mental, or physical in nature. A spiritual seeker, who aspires to attain self-realization or God realization, will not be troubled by nonfulfilment of his worldly desires. However, a seeker of material objects would never be satisfied, even when his worldly desires are fulfilled, because new desires crop up in his mind constantly. He will never be able to experience and appreciate the simplicity and blissfulness of the spiritual world and the Saints.

Human beings seek pleasure or pain according to their *prarabdha* carried forward from the past lives and this practice has been prevalent since the start of human civilization. We define pleasure and pain in accordance with our own perceptions. If someone, whether he has power and wealth or not, really wants to find a way to get rid of the worldly pains, he will have to seek refuge under a Sadguru.

Shirdi Sai Baba has asked His devotees to be satisfied with whatever God gives them. How can a person even imagine that all his wishes will be fulfilled in life? If that was so, Lord Rama and the Pandavas would not have suffered so much and for so long. How can any human being assert that he qualifies spiritually to have everything he desires in his possession? Many of our desires and dreams do not come true in life.

Q. **At times, a sense of despair overtakes a person when facing the worldly challenges. Is there a way to get out of this?**

A. Human beings suffer from a sense of despair when their desires do not get fulfilled, in spite of their best of efforts. This sense of despair is further accentuated when they visualise the impossibility of fulfilment of the desires in future also. In other words, desperation creeps into a person when some of his dreams do not actualize.

It is not wrong to have dreams, as much as it is not a virtue not to have dreams. The problem arises when a person expects all his desires to get fulfilled, which is not possible. If he accepts the fact that life is nothing but a mix of successes and failures, then he will not feel miserable when some, but not all, of his wishes get fulfilled. History is replete with examples of great and noble personalities who did not succeed in their ventures, some of which were noble. Hence, the acceptance of the middle path in life, as shown by the Perfect Masters, and also by the wise people, is the best course to follow. One should neither feel extremely happy and elated in success, nor feel extremely unhappy and dejected in failure. Success and failure are two sides of the same coin that will always exist as a reality in human life.

For the devotees of Shri Shirdi Sai Baba, I can only quote what Baba used to tell His devotees, "*Even if the whole world goes upside down (topsy-turvy), don't get perturbed. Just watch and see what happens next.*" With constant mental companionship and contemplation on Baba, our sorrows will definitely be reduced. The troubled mind will find solace if we regularly read Shri Sai Satcharita and constantly remember Baba. Hence, we should read more and more about Baba, contemplate on Him, chant His name, and sing bhajan and kirtanas, both in good times and in bad times.

Q. **How can a person get divine help for solving the mundane problems of life?**

A. In the ultimate analysis, the solution-giver of all the problems — material, mental, or spiritual — is God alone. It is the Divine Energy that creates the universe and sustains it in its totality. Human beings are like tiny particles floating in the ocean of the Divine Consciousness. Even the saints, who are completely detached from the sordid realities of the mundane earth, sometimes face problems and beseech God to grant them solutions.

God gives solutions to different souls through different mediums. The Sadguru is the most potent spiritual medium of God to solve the problems of the devotees. Shirdi Sai Baba has often said this.

> **Baba's Worship**
> Those who are fortunate and whose demerits have vanished; take to My worship. If you always say "Sai, Sai", I shall take you over the seven seas. Believe in these words and you will be certainly benefited. I do not need any paraphernalia of worship either, eight-fold or sixteen-fold. I rest there where there is full devotion.
> (Chapter 13, *Shri Sai Satcharita*)

His advent on earth was to solve the problems of His devotees and bring them solace. Sai Baba also spoke the following words for the happiness and welfare of his devotees.:

> **Efficacy of the Touch of Guru's Hand**
> There will never be any dearth or scarcity regarding food and clothes in My devotee's home. It is My special characteristic that I always look to and provide for the welfare of those devotees who worship Me wholeheartedly with their minds ever fixed on Me.
> (Chapter 6, *Shri Sai Satcharita*)

Q. It is mentioned in Shri Sai Satcharita that devotees afflicted with serious diseases like leprosy use to get cured by Sai Baba. Is it possible?

A. It is mentioned in Chapter 7 of Shri Sai Satcharita that many sick persons, including lepers, used to get cured by having the darshan of Baba. This may possibly be true because the writer of this book, Hemadpant, used to be a frequent visitor to Shirdi. He could have experienced such miraculous phenomenon himself.

This belief is further strengthened by the empirical evidence that is available. A devotee of Baba, by the name Bhagoji Shinde, is said to have been cured of leprosy due to Baba's kindness. Most of the devotees of Shirdi Sai Baba are aware that Bhagoji Shinde stayed in close proximity of Baba and he used to clean and bandage His injured hand every day.

Shri Sai Satcharita is replete with such incidents in which Baba cured devotees who were suffering from various types of mental and physical afflictions. Diseases like cholera, plague, eye and stomach problems, and even neuro problems used to be cured by Him. He is reported to have saved Shama, an ardent devotee, from the poison of a snake bite. When Mrs Khaparde, the wife of Dada Saheb Khaparde of Amravati, reported to Baba about her son's illness (plague), Baba helped her.

> **Khaparde's Son**
> Baba spoke kind and soft words to her, saying that the sky is beset with clouds; but they will melt and pass off and everything will be smooth and clear. So saying, He lifted His Kafni up to the waist and showed to all present, four fully developed buboes, as big as eggs, and said, "See, how I have to suffer for My devotees; their difficulties are Mine." (Chapter 7, *Shri Sai Satcharita*)

Q. Some devotees of Baba, at times, experience loneliness in life. What is the way out of such a situation?

A. I am of the view that no human being exists alone in life. A human being is a social creature who exists in the society and depends on others for his physical and mental needs. Further, I am yet to come across a person who is completely alone in life and yet exists in society. Feeling of such loneliness can be a temporary phase of mind as this is not the general rule.

However, in the case of the devotees of Shirdi Sai Baba, it can be different. Baba's devotees are emotionally linked with Him. Even if nobody is with them, they feel that Baba is there with them and around them. Shirdi Sai Baba had given the assurance to His devotees that even after His Samadhi, He would continue to help them in distress and would take care of them.

> **The Tomb Which Speaks**
>
> Baba said, "Believe Me, though I pass away, My bones in My tomb will give you hope and confidence. Not only Myself, but My tomb would be speaking, moving, and communicating with those who would surrender themselves wholeheartedly to Me. Do not be anxious that I would be absent from you. You will hear My bones speaking and discussing your welfare. But remember Me always, believe Me in heart and soul, and then you will be most benefited." (Chapter 25, Shri Sai Satcharita)

Therefore, whenever any devotee of Baba feels lonely, he should read Shri Sai Satcharita, worship Baba, listen to Sai Aarti and Bhajans, pay a visit to His temple, and meditate on Him. He should also discuss his problems with the other Sai devotees who are at the same devotional frequency. If a devotee holds on to Baba intensely, then even if he is mentally disconnected from the entire society, he will not feel lonely. I have seen this happening to a large number of devotees.

6

Dreams

Q. **What are dreams? Many devotees speak about their dream experience with Shirdi Sai Baba. What is your opinion?**

A. The series of thoughts, images, or emotions that play in our subconscious mind during sleep are known as dreams. The scope of dreams ranges from the ordinary to the surreal and most of the dreams have strange or unusual events. The dreamer does not and cannot control the events in the dream. Some dreams may be of a creative and spiritual nature, but these are extremely rare. Hindu spiritual science believes in communication through dreams between the Guru or Deity and the disciples or the devotees. Before His Maha Samadhi in 1918, many devotees from different places saw Baba in their dreams, in which Baba informed them about His impending departure. Chapter 29 of Shri Sai Satcharita, in particular, elucidates an example, that is, a dream in which a lady in a group of bhajan singers from Tamil Nadu saw Baba in the form of Lord Rama.

There is also a mention in Chapter 39 of Shri Sai Satcharita about Kaka Saheb Dixit and Shama, both having the same dream at the same time and at the same place at Dixit Wada at Shirdi. In the dream, Baba asked them to build a ward, housing a temple, at Shirdi. Even today, we hear from a large number of devotees, living in India and in foreign countries, about such occurrences in dreams pertaining to Baba. Reportedly, they see Baba in various places, in different moods, giving solutions to their problems, and even certain directions in order to save them from future troubles. For them, the purpose of such dreams, sooner or later, gets revealed. The Sadgurus or the Perfect Masters create dreams in the sleeping devotees by entering into their subconscious state of mind, in order to protect, help, and guide them in their life.

Construction of the Samadhi Mandir

Baba never talked, nor ever made any fuss about the things which He wanted to accomplish, but He so skilfully arranged the circumstances and surroundings that the people were surprised at the slow but sure results attained. The construction of the Samadhi Mandir is an instance in point. Shriman Bapusaheb Buti, the famous multimillionaire of Nagpur, lived in Shirdi with his family. Once, an idea arose in his mind that he should have a building of his own there. Sometime after this, while he was sleeping in Dixit Wada, he got a vision. Baba appeared in his dream and ordered him to build a Wada of his own with a temple. Shama, who was sleeping there, got also a similar vision. When Bapusaheb woke up, he saw Shama crying and asked him the reason. The latter replied that in his vision Baba came close to him and ordered distinctly, " 'Build the Wada with a temple. I shall fulfil the desires of all.' Hearing the sweet and loving words of Baba, I was overpowered with emotion, my throat was choked, my eyes were overflowing with tears, and I began to cry." Bapusaheb was surprised to see that both their visions tallied. (Chapter 39, *Shri Sai Satcharita*)

Yoga

Q. **So many references are found in Shri Sai Satcharita about yoga. What is the basis of yoga and who propounded it? Did Baba advise His devotees to practise Yoga?**

A. Patanjali, an Indian spiritual personality of the 2nd century B.C. is considered to be the founder and codifier of the system of yoga. His magnum opus, called *Patanjali Yoga Sutra*, covers the entire gamut of Yoga Sadhana developed by the Vedic Saints. The practice of yoga has been divided into eight parts. They are Yama, Niyama, Asana, Pranayama, Pratyahara, Dharana, Dhyana, and Kaivalya. Through the practice of yoga, a person can gain various subtle, occult, and spiritual powers. Salvation and oneness with God is its ultimate end.

Even though Baba was an adept in various yoga practices, He has reportedly forbidden His devotees to undergo the rigorous practices of Hatha Yoga. He has advised His devotees to merge their consciousness with His consciousness by contemplating on Him—with form or without form. He has advised the devotees to meditate on His physical form or on His formless reality.

Baba used to tell His devotees that there are many paths to God, of which He was one. He further advised the devotees to follow the path prescribed by Him. His method of spiritual training included a few components of Yoga Sadhana, but there is no reference to confirm that He ever asked His devotees to practice Yoga Sadhana rigorously.

8

God, Religion, Path, and Philosophy

Q. **To what extent is the human intelligence helpful towards the attainment of divine knowledge?**

A. Intelligence of the ordinary human beings is extremely limited for the purpose of spiritual evolution. It generally functions with a series of logic. It is impossible to attain complete knowledge, in any sphere of knowledge, in its entirety within a single life span.

The ignorance of any human being far exceeds his knowledge. That is why it is difficult for him to attain divine knowledge. In reality, human beings proceed very slowly in the path of spiritual knowledge, through years and decades of experience. The use of intelligence has to be shifted from the avoidable mundane matters and used for gaining divine knowledge when practicing an ethical standard of life.

Q **Why is it said that even *Devatas* aspire for a human form?**

A. Hinduism holds that a *Devata* has a subtle body and not a gross body like that of a human being. Each Devata is depicted to be the controller of a certain energy form of nature, for example, Agni Devata controls fire, Vayu Devata controls air, Jala Devata controls water, etc. It is not possible to perform the spiritual practices needed for salvation in a subtle body. The Devatas live in heaven and enjoy the pleasures of heaven, which is a place of enjoyment and not of atonement, penance, or of sadhana. Till there is *bhog*, that is, enjoyment, liberation is not possible. Only when *paapa* and *punya* are both exhausted that the true nature or the real form of the *jiva* is realized.

Both gross and subtle forms of spiritual practice are possible only by a human being and not by any Devata, who has a subtle body. Karma decides the path of the *jiva*, whether it is *paapa* karma or *punya* karma. Even *punya* karma contains a little of *paapa* in it and however terrible the *paapa* karma is, it also contains a bit of *punya*. According to the law of nature, everything on this earth must contain the opposites, for example, good and bad or day and night. That is why the soul has to take birth again and again due to *prarabdha* or in order to experience the fruits of good and bad actions of its past life. This takes a long period of time. The Sadgurus alone are capable of neutralizing the effects of the *prarabdha* of the disciples. They can help the devotees by giving proper direction to perform certain karmas which are necessary for spiritual evolution.

Because karma is the basis for liberation and karma is possible only in a gross human body, therefore even gods yearn for a gross human body. According to the Indian mythology, many Devatas, in the past, took human form in order to achieve liberation.

Q. **Why is the importance of human form emphasized repeatedly in the epics?**
A. The saints and realized souls hold that the human body is an instrument to realize God. We can perform spiritual practice and realize God with a gross human body. Devatas are unembodied souls or divine forces without a physical body. When a human being dies, he

becomes a disembodied soul or *preta*. Even the Devatas have to be born in a human form in order to realize God. This is the law of nature. That is why we must contemplate on the importance of our human birth. We have ascended to the stage of *manav yoni* or human form after passing through a long process of evolution.

Q. How should we look at various happenings of life from a spiritual point of view?

A. In order to have faith in God and spiritualism, we must understand the cause of happening of different incidents in life in an objective and comprehensive manner. Whatever happens within or around us, has to be understood in a wider perspective, spreading over multiple lives. We must try to understand the basic reasons behind all the happenings in life in a holistic manner and not as individual and unrelated incidents, creating happiness and unhappiness. Strong faith or belief cannot survive without such an understanding and this understanding cannot grow without strong faith or belief in God and Guru. Therefore, both these things are interdependent. Many times, human beings experience that an incident, which seemed to be adverse at the beginning, later turned out to be favourable and an incident which apparently seemed to be good becomes disastrous later. Therefore, we should try not to be completely shaken in adversity and become over-excited when something good happens in life.

Q. Why are human beings said to be the best creations of God on earth?

A. The reason is that human intelligence is more evolved when compared with the intelligence of all the other living species on earth. All other living beings are guided purely by animal instinct, whereas human beings are guided by intellect. The human race has intellectual consciousness, whereas the other species possess instinctive consciousness. It is because of his intellect that a human being has the capacity to control other living organisms on earth.

Humans are not only capable of controlling other living beings, but also have the capabilities of controlling various forces of nature. By controlling the elements of nature, humans use them in their favour, for example, electricity and radio waves, etc. Humans can laugh because they have the sense of critical analysis, which other creatures do not have.

The most important reason is that the human beings have the concept of and faith in God and try for God realization. None of the species have the intelligence even to think that there is an all pervading sovereign factor known as God. This makes the human race superior to all other creatures on earth.

Q. **It is said that a stable mind is an asset for spiritual evolution. Can you please comment on this?**

A. Human intellect emanates from the mind. The mind works within a limited boundary. Human beings are limited by their innate nature, karmic destiny known as *prarabdha*, experiences of the present life, and memory. We differentiate between what is good and what is evil, based on memories of our past experiences. However, the human mind and intelligence are highly volatile in nature and suffer from many limitations. The mind thinks of one thing as good at one moment and as bad at another moment. It is not possible to rely on such intelligence always. Hence, it is impossible to progress in the spiritual path with the help of such an unstable mind.

The edifice of devotion stands on the two pillars of love and faith for God. There is a difference between pure emotion and sheer emotionalism. Very often people think that being emotional is the same as nurturing pure emotion. Pure thoughts are those that are unblemished and can only be experienced when the mind is pious and stable. Emotion is like flowing water — wanton and uninhibited. Such a state of emotion can give personal pleasure but it is not of any use for universal welfare. Emotion must be supported by knowledge and wisdom.

When the mind is stable, certain virtues get rooted in the human being. To approach and get closer to the Guru, mental stability is needed. It is extremely difficult for a person with a fickle mind to progress in the spiritual path. Therefore, at the initial stages of spiritual sadhana, the Gurus put the disciples through a lot of rigorous and mental practices to increase their faith.

> In the year 1911, Shri Kasinath Upasani Maharaj came to Baba for his spiritual evolution and stayed at Shirdi for a few months. Thereafter, he carried on with his spiritual practices up to the year 1914 at a place called Sakori situated near Shirdi. During the period of his sadhana, he had to go through such humiliation and difficulties that no other human being ever faced during Baba's time. He was without food for more than a year and was physically assaulted by a quasi-lunatic person called Nanavali. The physical and mental tortures he received continuously were so hard that he even contemplated to commit suicide. Whenever, he would complain to Baba, Shri Sainath Maharaj used to advise him that the more pain he tolerated, the better would be his spiritual future.

Q. How can we attain divine bliss?
A. Divine bliss is not something that can be experienced in the manner in which most of the people imagine it to be or have read about it or have been told about it by some preachers. We have to put in a lot of effort, even to experience a glimpse of divine bliss. Saints and yogis

of yore used to perform sadhana during their entire lifetime in order to receive this divine bliss. Such an arduous effort can be compared with the difficult task of taking honey out of a honeycomb. First of all, some dry wood has to be burnt under the tree to produce smoke which would force the honeybees to rush out of the hive. Once the bees desert the honeycomb, only then it is possible to collect the honey. Similarly, on the spiritual front, we have to become something like the honeycomb and become devoid of all worldly desires and attachments. And then, burning oneself in the sacred fire of knowledge or *jnanagni*, we have to strive to get rid of negative qualities of anger, greed, ego, delusion, and ignorance. Only then can the smoke of devotion be produced. The web of worldly illusion and the sins of our past karma (*prarabdha*) are like honeybees — only the sacred fire of knowledge, penance, and austerity can remove these entanglements and lead to the ultimate experience of divine bliss. If we do not follow the correct spiritual path, the honeybees of illusion, ignorance, and delusion will keep torturing us and will deprive us of experiencing the serene feeling of divine bliss.

Q. Goddesses are worshipped in Hinduism and not in other religions. Is worshiping Goddesses the only divine path?

A. At first, we should understand the meaning of the word Goddess or the Devi in Hinduism. The meaning of the word *Devi* or *Daivi Shakti* is the same. The power of God is called *Daivi Shakti*. The male form of such Shakti is called Devata and the female form symbolizing such power is known as Devi. In reality, Brahma or the ultimate God is neither male nor female. Males and females have different characteristics, but Brahma is devoid of such attributes.

God, Religion, Path, and Philosophy

In Hinduism, the ten hands of Shri Durga symbolize the confluence of ten different powers of God for the purpose of destruction of the evil forces on earth. Whether such symbols are used in a religion or not, all living beings and non-living matter in this universe are controlled by certain divine powers.

In the past, Goddesses like Minerva, Artemis, and Eros used to be worshipped in the Greek civilization. It is not correct to say that Goddesses are worshipped only in Hinduism.

Q. At times, some devotees display their pride in being a devotee of a Guru or a deity. Is not such pride detrimental to spiritual evolution?

A. We should never be proud of our devotion and consider ourselves to be superior to others because we happen to be the devotee of a Guru or a deity. When all are equal in the eyes of God, how can we consider ourselves as a superior devotee to others? Who is to decide about the quality of devotion of a devotee? Should it be done by the devotee himself, or is better left to the Guru to decide?

The spiritual path is extremely complex and difficult to follow. Advancement on the path can be made only by following the method suggested by the Sadguru, with humility, faith, and patience. Humility comes from the realization that a human being is an insignificant entity in the vast universe.

Some people always seek glory. Some people desire to have knowledge. Until the greater virtues like willingness to serve, love, sacrifice, and humility are developed in a human being, his advancement on the spiritual path is not easy. No one can reach the peak of the Himalayas just by taking a vow to do so, even if he repeats the vow a thousand times a day. Patience, single-mindedness, self-confidence, and hard work are required. It is for this reason that Baba used to ask for the two coins of shraddha and saburi as dakshina from devotees. It is difficult to sustain shraddha (faith) without saburi (patience) and vice versa. Assertion of devotional ego only brings in delay in the process of spiritual evolution.

Q. It is said that a spiritual seeker faces a lot of difficulties in life. Why is this so?

A. Those who sincerely wish to take the spiritual path, have to think and act differently from others who merely want to excel in the world of materialism while following the norms of worldly conduct. For example, if a greedy person is asked to part with 25 per cent of his earnings in the name of God or distribute it among the poor, he will feel extremely distressed. However, if he has some faith in God, he may be propelled to sacrifice a little.

It is not wise to assume that spiritual journey is synonymous to a journey that is full of pain and grief. Those who get entangled in the web of worldly desires generally experience much greater grief and misery. While making a journey along the spiritual path, we have to follow the ethical principles prescribed by religion and administered by the Guru. Even when doing so, the devotee will face the same mundane problems that he used to face earlier. He will have to be more tolerant and hard working to face the problems because he has to follow the prescribed ethical standards. People around him may criticize him and even oppose him for his ethical behaviour. As he will gradually evolve during the spiritual journey, his perception about pain and pleasure will gradually change. The journey along the spiritual path will steadily reduce the agonies of the worldly entanglements, material hindrances, and, consequently, the pain.

Sometimes, ignorant people, observing the trials and tribulations faced by the saints and the holy souls, start feeling sorry for them. Such people are just looking at the surface of things. True saints are free from worldly bondage and illusions. They are perpetually in a state of bliss. They do not experience pain and pleasure like an ordinary mortal, because they possess complete control over their mind, intellect, and senses. Shri Shirdi Sai Baba used to maintain this state of mind even when solving the serious, mundane problems of His devotees.

Q. Is there any difference between religion and devotion?

A. There is a basic difference between the two and this can be illustrated by using the example of a cat and a dog. As is generally observed, following a religion can be compared with the love of a cat for the home in which it lives. Everyone needs a home for protection, and religion gives that protection. It is said, a cat loves the house of the owner more than the owner himself. As long as the home gives it the comforts and food, it does not make much difference to the cat if the master is at home or is away. On the other hand, the dog loves the master more than the house where it lives. The dog follows the master wherever he goes. It has been found that, at times, the dog does not take food or drink when the master is absent. There are many reports which show that after the demise of the master, the dog did not survive for long.

A human being can love God even without belonging to any religion. The dog symbolizes devout devotion, whereas the cat symbolizes religion, if the comparison has to be made in general terms.

Q. In our busy life, is it possible to take some small steps to evolve ourselves?

A. There are many small steps that we can take for self evolution. Such steps can be in terms of doing certain things and in not doing certain things. First, we should not hurt anyone deliberately, create problems for others due to our negative thoughts, use bad language, or precipitate unkind actions. The negative thoughts of a person can cause considerable harm to himself and others in the long term. As far as possible, we should try to give happiness to others, even if it is in small measures, in whichever way it is possible to do so. If someone approaches us in distress, we can give encouragement, mental support, and a little help, if possible. To a hungry person, we can offer food. We can learn to give happiness to others in simple ways. Before rejecting a request for help, we should think of how much happiness we can bring to the suffering person. As per Sai Baba's advice, we should not speak rudely to a person asking for help. This attitude should be annihilated. We can get rid of ego only by striving continuously to get rid of it. Besides human beings, we should not give pain but give love to animals and other living beings. We can get rid of negative thoughts and instincts only through constant practice. God helps those who help themselves. The answer to this question can be clearly found in the following anecdote:

> Kasinath Upasani Maharaj was cooking his food at Khandoba temple and, naturally, wanted to take the food to his Guru, Sai Baba, and to get back the same or rather a part of it as prasad from Him to eat. While he was cooking his food, a black dog was watching and even when he took the food towards Sai's Masjid, it followed him part of the way and suddenly disappeared. When the dog was first present and anxiously looking for food,

> Upasani, with his orthodox ideas, thought it would be absurd to give that low creature, a dog, any food before offering it to God and before men ate (for that was against orthodox ideas). So, he did not give any food to the dog. But when he went, in the hot sun at noon, with his food to Sai Baba, Baba asked him, "What have you come for?" Kasinath said, "To bring you my naivedya." "Why did you come all the way here in the sun? I was there," Baba said. Kasinath said that there was none but a black dog there. Baba said, "I was that black dog. So, as you refused to give me food there, I am not going to take this food." So, Upasani returned that day bitterly repenting his orthodox frame of mind refusing to give food first to the dog. (Chapter 6, Part II, *Life of Sai Baba*, Narasimha Swami, p. 410)

Q. **The word *atmasakshatkar* has been repeatedly mentioned in Shri Sai Satcharita. What does it mean?**

A. This Sanskrit word means self-realization or God realization. Many people also interpret it as salvation and emancipation.

The human soul is like a drop of water in the unlimited and all-pervading ocean of divine consciousness. Even when this drop of divine consciousness gets embodied in a human form and gets embroiled with the worldly affairs called maya, it does not lose its innate divine nature. When a person goes through a series of arduous and long-drawn yogic practices, he experiences the pristine nature of his soul and rediscovers himself. It can also be said that he realizes the fundamental nature of his soul, which is divine. When he experiences God in his soul and finds no difference between his soul and the Over-Soul, only then can he be said to have experienced *atmasakshatkar*.

Shri Shirdi Sai Baba's basic aim was to give *atmasakshatkar* to His devotees. The birth and death cycles of a human being come to end when he experiences *atmasakshatkar*.

Q. Some people have told me that they experienced God in various ways. Two persons have told me that they have experienced God. I have been an ardent devotee of Baba for the last 20 years but have not got any such experience. I feel very depressed. Can you please help me?

A. Spiritual truth or reality is not what we generally conceptualize it to be. When walking on the path of spiritualism, often people misinterpret their petty experiences, excitements, dream stories, imaginations, and emotional upsurges as spiritual realization, whereas it is not so. I have met a number of people who think that they have experienced spiritual reality because of a few dreams or sparks of light they saw during sleep or meditation. Each person gets spiritual experiences according to his spiritual practices, and eventually, starts experiencing the ultimate reality of God. When he reaches the height of spiritual consciousness, he receives divine revelation as the ultimate reality. What he experiences cannot be described fully in any words because it is the ultimate experience. Such an experience is attained by human beings who have undergone arduous and long spells of spiritual practice under the guidance of a Sadguru. It is the Guru who, ultimately, has with him the capability to realize truth. Please go through the anecdotes written in Chapter 16 and 17 of Shri Sai Satcharita pertaining to a greedy businessman who came to Baba for getting Brahmagyan and that too within a few hours.

Fast Track Brahmagyan

There was a rich gentleman (unfortunately his name and whereabouts are not mentioned) who was very prosperous in his life. He had amassed a large quantity of wealth, houses, field, and lands and had many servants and dependents. When Baba's fame reached his ears, he said to a friend that he was not in want of anything and so he would go to Shirdi and ask Baba to give him Brahmagyan which, if he got, would certainly make him happier. His friend dissuaded him, saying, "It is not easy to know Brahman, and especially so for an avaricious man like you, who is always engrossed in wealth, wife, and children. Who can satisfy you in your quest of Brahmagyan, when you won't give away even a pice in charity?"

Not minding his friend's advice, the gentleman engaged a return-journey tonga and came to Shirdi. He went to the Masjid, saw Sai Baba, fell at His feet and said, "Baba, hearing that You show the Brahman to all who come over here without any delay, I have come here all the way from my distant place. I am much fatigued by the journey and if I get the Brahman from You, my troubles will be well-paid and rewarded." Baba then replied, "Oh, My dear friend, do not be anxious, I shall immediately show you the Brahman; all My dealings are in cash and never on credit. So many people come to Me, and ask for wealth, health, power, honour, position, cure of diseases, and other temporal matters. Rare is the person who comes here to Me and asks for Brahmagyan. There is no dearth of persons asking for worldly things, but as persons interested in spiritual matters are very rare, I think it a lucky and auspicious moment when persons like you come and press Me for Brahmagyan.

So, I show to you, with pleasure, the Brahman with all its accompaniments and complications."

Saying this, Baba started to show him the Brahman. He made him sit there and engaged him in some other talk or affairs and thus made him forget his question for the time being. Then He called a boy and told him to go to one Nandu Marwari and get from him a hand-loan of five rupees. The boy left and returned immediately, saying that Nandu was absent and his house was locked. Then Baba asked him to go to Bala grocer and get the loan from him. This time also the boy was unsuccessful. This process was repeated again twice or thrice, with the same result.

Sai Baba was, as we know, the living and moving Brahman Incarnate. Then, someone may ask, "Why did He want a paltry sum of five rupees and why did He try hard to get it on loan?" Actually, He did not want that sum at all. He must have known well that Nandu and Bala were absent and seems to have adopted this procedure as a test for the seeker of Brahman.

The gentleman had a bundle of currency notes in his pocket and if he was really earnest, he would not have sat quietly as a mere onlooker when Baba was frantically trying to get this small sum as a loan. He knew that Baba would keep His word and repay the debt and that the sum wanted was insignificant. Still, he could not make up his mind and give the money. Such a man wanted from Baba the greatest thing in the world, that is, the Brahmagyan! Any other man, who really loved Baba, would have at once given the five rupees, instead of sitting passively.

> It was otherwise with this gentleman. He advanced no money, nor did he sit silently, but began to be impatient, as he was in a haste to return and implored Baba saying, "Oh Baba, please show me the Brahman soon." Baba replied, "Oh, My dear friend, did you not understand all the procedure that I went through, sitting in this place, for enabling you to see the Brahman? It is, in short, this. For seeing Brahman, one has to give five things, that is, surrender five things: (1) Five Pranas (vital forces), (2) Five senses (five of action and five of perception), (3) Mind, (4) Intellect, and (5) ego." This path of Brahmagyan or self-realization is "as hard as it is to tread on the edge of a razor". (Chapter 16 and 17, *Shri Sai Satcharita*)

Q. **It is said that rarely does a human being experience the Ultimate Spiritual Truth. Why is it limited to a few Saints and Sadgurus?**

A. Although human beings have the potential to realize God, only a few have the capacity to truly strive for it and achieve it. Spiritual truth and experience dawns on a seeker only with the grace of God and through the medium of the Sadguru. However, to be able to receive and retain such divine experience, the recipient should be worthy of it. Divine love can't be kindled in the heart as easily as we imagine. Sadhana, spreading over a few lifetimes, is required.

It is an illusion to think that we can experience spiritual reality merely by visiting temples, worshipping deities, displaying emotional feats, and conducting a few pujas. Wholehearted sadhana is necessary, in addition to the compassion of the Sadguru and the worthiness of the spiritual aspirant. If the soil is not fertile and ready for cultivation, what is the use of sowing a seed in it? Creating a fertile land requires efforts of many lifetimes.

This process of preparation may be called sadhana. If the soil used for the plants is of a poor quality, then some of the seeds will germinate, but they will not grow fully to become good trees. At times, it is seen that when the mind is not well-trained and strong, even a spark of divine energy can make an amateur practitioner lose his psychological balance. Training and control of the mind are the basic requirements for spiritual evolution. According to Hindu belief, it may take a few lives to evolve to this state. Only a few Saints and Sadgurus have the perseverance to work towards this goal with devotion.

Q. **Is the path of devotion (bhakti) better than the path of knowledge (gyan) and karma?**

A. According to spiritual philosophy, the concepts of devotion, knowledge, and karma cannot be considered in isolation. They are inter-woven. They have been defined separately just for a clearer understanding of the devotee. The paths of gyan (knowledge) and karma (actions) are not complete in themselves, whereas the path of devotion is complete in itself. This is the reason because of which so many illiterate people have become saints but highly educated and knowledgeable people belonging to the intellectual world could not rise to that spiritual status. Sant Gyaneshwar, Tukaram, Shri Ramakrishna Paramahamsa, and Shri Sai Baba of Shirdi had no formal education. This does not mean that gyan and karma should be given up for the sake of devotion. Gyan and karma are necessary steps in the path of devotion.

The main aim of spiritualism is to realize God through the path of devotion only. Devotion ultimately leads to self-realization and gives direct knowledge. A devotee who is emotionally devotional tries to do his best for the satisfaction of the Guru or the deity. He is a highly motivated soul who can perform more than what gyan or karma yogis can do. In short, if devotion is taken as a vast ocean, then gyan and karma can be taken as two big rivers merging in it and, thereby, feeding it. Shrimad Bhagavat narrates in detail about Raj Yoga, Karma Yoga, Gyan Yoga, and Bhakti Yoga.

Q. Can God be realized only through the Bhakti Marg?
A. Realization of God purely through the Bhakti Marg can be achieved by one person in crores. This can be attained due to the good *prarabdha* and *samskaras* of the past lives and by the grace of the Guru and God. Most devotees, saints, yogis, *munis*, and sadhus progress on the spiritual path by resorting to a combination of bhakti, gyan, and karma. Devotion gives direct knowledge, and the knowledge thus gained further strengthens devotion. Will power of the practitioner also gets strengthened in the process. With the increase in will power, the power of actions, or karma, also increases manifold. If truly devotional souls improve their gyan, then their progress will be faster. Most of our saints adopted this Gyan-Bhakti Marg or the path of devotion, combined with knowledge.

> Although Baba advocated, day and night, the greatness of knowledge above everything else, yet He generally advised the devotees to follow the path of devotion. He would stress the importance of the path of knowledge by comparing it to a *ramphal*. The path of devotion, he said, was like savouring a *sitaphal*, which is easily accessible and yet sweet and delicious. Devotion is the sitaphal, bright and clear. Knowledge is a perfectly ripened ramphal, each more juicy and delectable than the other and deliciously fragrant. (Chapter 19, *Shri Sai Satcharita*, Translated by Indira Kher)

> Baba: Gyan marga is like *ramphal*. Bhakti marga is like *sitaphal* (custard apple), easy to deal with and very sweet. The pulp of the *ramphal* is inside and difficult to get at. *Ramphal* should ripen on the tree and plucked when ripe. If it falls on the ground, it gets spoiled. So, if a *gyani* falls, he is ruined—even for a gyani there is the danger of a fall, for example, by a little negligence or carelessness.
> (*Sri Sai Baba's Charters and Sayings* by Narasimha Swami, p. 25)

Q. What sort of bhava has the maximum importance for the devotees of Baba?

A. Bhakti creates the purest form of emotional upsurge in the heart. Guru Bhakti has nine forms of expression—listening about the Guru, worshipping the Guru, serving the Guru, singing the glory of the Guru, chanting the name of the Guru, prostrating before the Guru, friendship with the Guru, surrendering to the Guru, and remembering the Guru. If a person practices any one of the three forms of Bhakti perfectly, then he makes spiritual progress. If a devotee follows any one out of the nine forms of devotions, then it spontaneously connects him with the other eight.

As mentioned in Shri Sai Satcharita, Megha, a simple but astute devotee, used to walk to Godavari river daily to bring water to give a bath to Baba. Dasa Bhava, or the devotee's role of being a servant to Guru, is said to be the best bhava, because it is based solely on the desire to serve the Guru. There is no place for ego or desire for any type of personal achievement. The servant remains fully surrendered to his Master. He is always eager to do his best for his Master. His only aim in life is to render service to the Guru. The Guru also takes full responsibility to protect the disciple and provide him with his requirements.

Anantrao Patankar

A gentleman from Pune, by the name Anantrao Patankar, wished to see Baba. He came to Shirdi and had Baba's darshan. His eyes were appeased and he was much pleased. He fell at Baba's feet. After performing proper worship, he said to Baba, "I have read a lot, studied Vedas, Vedantas, and Upanishads and heard all the Puranas, but still I have not got any peace of mind; so I think that all my reading was useless. Simple, ignorant, devout persons are better than me. Unless the mind becomes calm, all book-learning is of no avail. I have heard from many people that you easily give peace of mind to so many people by your mere glance and playful word. So I have come here. Please take pity on me and bless me." Then Baba told him a parable, which was as follows:

Parable of Nine Balls of Stool (Navadha Bhakti)

"Once a *saudagar* (merchant) came here. Before him a mare passed her stool (nine balls of stool). The merchant, intent on his quest, spread the end of his *dhotar* and gathered all the nine balls in it, and thus he got concentration (peace) of mind."

Patankar could not make out the meaning of this story. So he asked Ganesh Damodar, who was also called Dada Kelkar, "What does Baba mean by this?" Dada Kelkar replied, "I, too, do not know all that Baba says and means, but at His inspiration I say what I come to know. The mare is God's grace and the nine balls excreted are the nine forms or types of bhakti, that is, (1) Shravana (Hearing); (2) Kirtana (Praying); (3) *Smarana* (Remembering); (4) *Padasevana* (resorting to the feet); (5) *Archana* (Worship); (6) Namaskara (Bowing); (7) *Dasya* (Service); (8) *Sakhyatva*

(Friendship); and (9) *Atmanivedana* (surrender of the self). If any of these is faithfully followed, Lord Hari will be pleased and manifest Himself in the home of the devotee. All the sadhanas, that is, *japa* (vocal worship), *tapa* (penance), yoga practice and studying the scriptures and expounding them are quite useless unless they are accompanied by bhakti, that is, devotion. Knowledge of the Vedas or fame as a great gyani and mere formal bhajan (worship) are of no avail. What is wanted is loving devotion. Consider yourself as the merchant or seeker after the truth and be anxious and eager like him to collect or cultivate the nine types of devotion. Then you will attain stability and peace of mind."

Next day, when Patankar went to Baba for salutation, he was asked whether he collected the "nine balls of stool". Patankar said that he, being a poor fellow, should first be graced by Baba and then they will be easily collected. Then Baba blessed and comforted him, saying that he would attain peace and welfare. After hearing this, Patankar became overjoyed and happy. (Chapter 21, *Shri Sai Satcharita*)

Four Grains

Baba: A person rode on a camel which passed excreta. I gathered all the excreta and ate it up. My belly was puffed up and swollen. I felt listless. Then the rider took pity upon me. He gave me four grains of Bengal Gram (cana, Cicer arietinum) and I ate them and drank water. Then my vehement turbulence ceased. My swollen belly subsided. Now thereafter it will be cured. (*Sri Sai Baba's Charters and Sayings* by Narasimha Swami, p. 276)

Megha

Baba's work on Megha was purely internal. Baba did not give any oral instructions at all. But by internal change,

Megha became the most remarkable bhakta of Sai Baba, whom he considered really as Siva. Megha, being a hardy man, would go daily to Godavari—which is locally called Ganga, five miles away from Shirdi on route to Kopergaon station, bring Ganga water, and pour it on the head of Siva, Siva being Sai Baba.

Shri R. B. Purandhare, an *ankita* of Baba, mentions one *chamatkar* (miracle) of Baba. In his anxiety to pour Ganga water on Baba, Megha had brought a whole pot of it. Baba told him, "*Arre*, the head is the chief thing," *sarvasya gatrasya sirah pradhanam*, "so put a few drops on the head and that will suffice." But the impetuousness of Megha's bhakti made him pick up the whole pot and turn it upside down over Baba's head. Strangely, not a drop of water fell on Baba's body. The whole pot of water fell on the head, without touching His body. So, just as Siva had tied up Ganga in His own hair, Baba also used His head for retaining and throwing away the water so as not to touch His body or clothes. Megha was treated by Baba very kindly and Baba suited Himself to Megha's preferences. (Chapter 7, Part III, *Life of Sai Baba* by Narasimha Swami, p. 554)

After continuous service of Baba for many years, doing regular worship and aarti every noon and evening, Megha passed away in 1912. Then, Baba passed His hands over his corpse and said, "This was a true devotee of Mine." Baba also ordered that, at His own expense, the usual funeral dinner should be given to the Brahmins and this order was carried out by Kaka Saheb Dixit. (Chapter 28, *Shri Sai Satcharita*)

Q. How can we know which of the karmas of the present life will become *prarabdha* of the future lives?

A. Sometimes, unexpected events taking place in life are said to be *prarabdha karmas*. For example, a serious disease, an accident, or sudden death can happen. When something like this happens suddenly (even though, to the best of our knowledge, we did not do anything wrong in the current life to deserve it), then we hold it to be *prarabdha karma*.

Despite having the knowledge to differentiate between good and evil, when we deliberately commit something that we should not have done, then we accumulate adverse *karmic prarabdha*. Similarly, if we perform noble acts, following the instructions of the Guru or the scriptures, it creates positive *karmic prarabdha*. Every act committed by a human being, every day, throughout his life, does not necessarily take the shape of *karmic prarabdha*. The effects of most of such activities get exhausted immediately or during the lifetime. Let us take the example of a person who goes to a shop and purchases certain items from the shopkeeper. After selecting the items, he purchases them by making payment to the shopkeeper. With this, the one-time transaction between the buyer and the seller is over. Neither does the shop owner remember all the customers, nor does the customer remember all the shop owners whose shops he visits. However, later, if the buyer finds that the owner of the shop from which he procured an item has given him a defective product, then he feels sad and cheated. He returns to the shop owner and asks him to change the defective product for a good one. If the shop owner repents and replaces with a good product, then no ill feeling is harboured in the mind of the customer. However, if the shopkeeper refuses to do so, the customer feels hurt and a *karma prarabdha* takes place. Under rules of *karma prarabdha*, the shopkeeper has to pay for it in this life or in the next one.

If each and every action committed by an individual during his lifetime, and connected with the thousands of other human beings, were to become *karma prarabdha*, then all human beings will have to go through unending cycles of births and deaths just to repay the karmic debts. To qualify to become a karma prarabdha, there has to be an unmitigated, material, or emotional debt between the debtor and the debtee. Borrowing money from a person with a promise to return and not returning it during the life time creates a material debt. A relationship of friendship based on love, or enmity based on hatred creates the karmic debt known as *prarabdha*.

This is why Rishis, Munis, Gurus, and Parents always emphasize on the importance of the practice of *sadachar* or moral conduct.

Q. Do human beings always welcome pleasure and avoid pain?

A. According to the theory of Pleasure and Pain propounded in the western philosophy, what gives pleasure is good and desirable and what gives pain is evil and, therefore, undesirable. Such an approach to life always inspires us to seek pleasure and avoid pain. A person who follows such a theory becomes a seeker of pleasure and becomes intolerant to pain.

It is not possible to realize the limitless and universal God without transcending the limits of the pleasure and pain that human beings generally experience. If a person maintains perfect mental equilibrium in the face of pleasure or pain, then he becomes a saint and realizes God. This is the true path to be followed, even if we do not have any desire of becoming a saint. We should try not to be over-excited by pleasure and depressed when in pain.

Factors creating happiness and unhappiness are like the two sides of a coin and they will always play their role in every human being's life. We must experience both to realize the true meaning of human life.

Q. What should be the ideal state of our consciousness?

A. The Sadgurus, saints, and the scriptures have advised that the consciousness of the human beings should be pure and simple to the extent possible. If a person truly wants to have direct vision of the universal form of God, then he should try to cleanse the inventory of the mind, which contains old memories, experiences, and strongly-rooted convictions. Otherwise, on the vast canvas of our consciousness, in place of a picture of the universe and God, a limited picture will get painted.

Shirdi Sai Baba's entire focus was on purifying the minds of His devotees. He used to keep an eye on the thoughts of all his devotees very closely and advise them suitably from time to time.

> Baba said: To get the knowledge (realization) of the self, Dhyana (meditation) is necessary. If you practice it continuously, the *vrittis* (thoughts) will be pacified. Being quite desire-less, you should meditate on the Lord, Who is in all the creatures. And when the mind is concentrated, the goal will be achieved. Meditate always on My formless nature, which is knowledge incarnate, consciousness, and bliss. If you cannot do this, meditate on My Form from top to toe as you see here night and day. As you go on doing this, your *vrittis* will concentrate on one point and the distinction between the Dhyata (meditator), Dhyana (act of meditation), Dhyeya (this meditated upon) will be lost and the meditator will be one with the Consciousness and be merged in the Brahman. (Chapters 18 and 19, *Shri Sai Satcharita*)

Q. **If all the living beings have to walk on the spiritual path and get salvation, then why is this path shrouded with so much mystery?**

A. This question is based on two assumptions. The first assumption is that all the living beings existing on earth will eventually tread along the spiritual path towards salvation. The second assumption is that the spiritual path is mysterious. Among the living beings, there are the lower species, as well as human beings. According to Hindu belief, even animals like cats and dogs can evolve to higher levels of consciousness after being born many numbers of times. Darwin also believed in the process of evolution, if not in the theory of reincarnation. Darwin's theory has not been found to be flawless.

There does not exist any theory which can prove that all creatures will necessarily tread the spiritual path towards salvation. History and Anthropology prove that, in the past, many species got destroyed on this earth due to environmental changes and natural calamities. Only the human race survived these catastrophes and evolved.

The human race, in the course of evolution, has been able to realize the existence of a Supreme Power called God and realize His role and His powers. The human race, at the initial stage of its evolution, did not have any concept about the existence of an Omnipotent, Omniscient, and Omnipresent God, who is full of compassion. Only a few human beings or evolved souls could realize God during the course of their lives. Most of the human beings on earth could surely evolve in this way if the earth were to become immortal. The earth, along with all its living and non-living elements, will vanish during the *pralaya*. Hence, only a small number of human beings will truly enter into the spiritual path within the lifetime of the earth and not all.

The spiritual path is a mystery for most of the people who are not able to unravel the complexities of the laws of nature that exist within and around the universe. But it is not a mystery for the yogis and the Gurus who have learnt to use such knowledge for the good of the society. Radio waves were a mystery till Marconi discovered them and utilized them for radio telegraphy. However, for the people who don't have access to such secrets of nature, they will remain a mystery. Science will unearth many more mysteries in future, as it has done in the past. A true spiritual practitioner can also unravel the mysteries.

Q. If God is one, then why are there many methods of worship and so many different religions?

A. Shirdi Sai Baba used to say, "There are many paths leading to God. One of the path leads from this place," meaning, from Shirdi.

In the written history of human civilization, it is found that people of different civilizations, at different periods of time, have created different methods of worship, depending on the prevalent social and cultural environment in which they lived. Such socio-cultural conditions undergo change from time to time. That is why the different religions created by the Incarnations also came under change during later periods of time and got divided into various sects and groups. Hinduism has Shaivaites, Vaishnavites, Saktyas, and many other sects. In the Muslim religion, there are the Shias and Sunnis, and Christianity has the Catholics and Protestants, etc. This is a reality which human civilization has created and accepted. In future, if any new religion takes birth, it will also go through the same process. In spite of such variations in approach to the worship of God, the same God exists and He continues to be worshipped throughout the world. A real lover of God, or one who has realized God, rises above the limitations of the organized religions. For a realized soul, love of God becomes the worship of God.

Swami Vivekananda made a profound statement, which is very pertinent in this context. In his concluding speech at the World Parliament of Religions at the World Trade Fair at Chicago on the September 27, 1893, he said:

"Each must assimilate the spirit of others and preserve his individuality and grow according to his own law of growth." This is relevant for spiritualism, for the law of growth of the inner self. This is also relevant for the peaceful existence of different religions on earth.

Q. **Wise men prescribe that we must maintain constant company of the noble and learned souls. What is the benefit of this?**

A. It is said, a man is known by the company he keeps. This also implies that the society gives value to a person and it also gives value to his companions. It is expected that in a human relationship, both sides should, as far as possible, have similar attitudes or habits. There is no doubt that bad company leads to the evil play of thoughts, leading to evil actions and noble company generates noble thoughts, leading to noble activities. At Shirdi, many ordinary and unknown villagers like Tatya, Shama, Mhalsapati, and others became famous due to the company of a divine and noble soul like Baba.

This question has been answered in Chapter 10 of Shri Sai Satcharita. The relevant portion is given below:

> You may do or attend to your worldly duties, but give your mind to Sai and His stories and then He is sure to bless you. This is the easiest path but why do all not take to it? The reason is that without God's grace, we do not get the desire to listen to the stories of saints. With God's

grace, everything is smooth and easy. Hearing the stories of the saints is, in a way, keeping their company.

The importance of the company of saints is very great. It removes our body-consciousness and egoism, destroys completely the chain of our birth and death, cuts asunder all the knots of the heart, and takes us to God, Who is pure Consciousness. It certainly increases our non-attachment to sense-objects, and makes us quite indifferent to pleasures and pains, and leads us on the spiritual path. If you have no other sadhana, such as uttering God's name, worship, or devotion, etc., but if you take refuge in them (saints) wholeheartedly, they will carry you off safely across the ocean of worldly existence.

It is for this reason that the saints manifest themselves in this world. A man is known by the company he keeps. The close companions of a person play a great role in conditioning the thought process of the individual. If these people are of a low and evil temperament, then the thoughts of the person will become low and evil. However, if he keeps the company of the holy and saintly persons, then his thoughts will become noble and lofty. This is why it is advised to read and listen to the life history of the saints. (Chapter 10, *Shri Sai Satcharita*)

Q. **What is Hinduism and what is its future?**
A. Hinduism and the Hindu way of life are more than five thousand years old. Hinduism should not be visualized simply as a religion. Through this period of history, the Hindus created a powerful culture which permeates every aspect of their existence. They painted their way of life on the vast canvas of culture, for happiness and stability. The Vedic and Post-Vedic philosophy and

practices of the Hindus, and also the Indian system of yoga, has gained international popularity and acceptance.

Hinduism cannot be defined simply as a religion in the strictest sense of the term. Hinduism is a way of life. This religion, as a way of life, has gone through various changes, as required by the insurgent situations of time. Given the unprecedented ethos of the present day global changes—political, economic, cultural, and even environmental—it becomes highly relevant to muse on the future shape of Hinduism. Since the Hindu way of life is highly tolerant to other religious cultures, it has the capabilities to absorb the invading cultures and yet retain its identity. In the past, when many civilizations and cultures in the world were closed in nature, Hinduism was ever open. In the future, with the invasion of modern science and technology, the world will become an open stage. Hinduism, as a way of life, will be greatly benefited by it and will, perhaps, lead the world.

9

The Master and the Disciples

Q. Why are there so many different types of Gurus?

A. There are many types and many levels of Gurus in the Hindu religion such as the *Kul Guru, Vidya Guru, Mantra Guru, Shiksha Guru,* and *Varna Guru,* who deal with different aspects of a person's life. In the same way, there are different levels of Gurus in the spiritual world. Besides the Sadgurus, nobody else has attained the state of *Purna Brahma*. This is so because only the Sadgurus have achieved the state of *sat-chit-ananda*. Other Gurus have limited capabilities and standards. They can impart spiritual education in accordance with their capabilities and can become a medium for imparting initial training to a disciple before the disciple comes to the Sadguru. Such spiritual Gurus in Hinduism are known by different names, such as muni, yogi, santh, sadhu, and many more. Whoever has received the shelter of a Sadguru need not search for any other Guru. He will achieve both temporal and spiritual benefits in life through the medium of the Sadguru, who has the highest divine capabilities. If a person accepts the other Gurus as Sadguru, then this will be his failing.

Abdul was a resident of Nanded. Sai Baba appeared in the dream of Abdul's *murshid* (that is, his teacher or Guru), Fakir Amiruddin. Baba put two mangoes in his

> hands and asked him to send Abdul to Shirdi. Fakir gave the mangoes to Abdul and asked him to go to Shirdi. When Abdul reached Shirdi, Baba welcomed him saying, "My crow has come," and directed him to devote himself entirely to His service. (Chapter 6, Part II, *Devotees Experiences of Sri Sai Baba* by Narasimha Swami, p. 152)

This incident indicates that the Sadguru can direct the other Gurus to act according to His wishes, which they follow.

Q. What is the secret and subtle role played by the Sadgurus for the spiritual evolution of the disciple?

A. The subtle power of the Sadguru works in so many ways that it is difficult to explain them all in detail. In short, a Sadguru plays His divine role at different levels, at different places, and at different points of time in the life of the devotee. In the ultimate analysis, it has been found that it is the Guru who attracts the disciples towards Him. For this, He alone chooses the time and method. Such power of attraction of the Guru reaches the devotee in the form of thought waves. The disciple becomes overjoyed and excited and gets attracted towards Him. As a result, he becomes eager to meet the Sadguru. Due to the newly evoked feeling of purity in his heart, he yearns to come closer to the Guru. Thereafter, a situation gets created which pulls the devotee to the Guru. Sometimes, the Guru also sends a message to the disciple or waits for his arrival. Shri Ramakrishna Paramahamsa used to wait anxiously for Shri Vivekananda. Shri Sainath Maharaj also had to wait for the arrival of Nana Saheb Chandorkar.

When such a relationship gets established, the Guru always keeps the devotee in His focus wherever He be. The Guru, who is ever aware of the past, present, and the future of the disciples, starts to protect him in various ways. The Sadguru does so in order to create a favourable condition, both material and mental, for the spiritual evolution of the disciple. He also protects the disciple from the dangers that he faces.

Nana was climbing the Harischandra Hill on a hot summer day. After he had gone some distance, he felt very thirsty and quietly sat on a huge slab and exclaimed, "If Baba were here, He would surely give me water to slake my thirst!" At Shirdi, Sai Baba spoke out immediately, in the presence of some devotees, "Hello, Nana is very thirsty. Should We not give him a handful of water?"

Soon after Nana made his exclamation about Baba, a Bhil was seen coming down the hill towards them. Nana accosted him and said, "Hello! I am thirsty; can I get some water to drink?" The Bhil said, "What! You ask for water! Under the very slab of rock on which you are seated, there is water." Nana's subordinates and friends who were with him immediately set about lifting the slab after Nana moved aside. Lo and behold! There was a palm-ful of water on that rock, just the quantity that is necessary to save a man from fiery thirst. Nana drank that water, and his thirst was gone. He was able to climb higher up and complete his pilgrimage. (Chapter 2, Part II, *Life of Sai Baba* by Narasimha Swami, p. 255)

One day at Shirdi, Baba made the dolorous *sankha* sound (indicative of coming death) and said "Hello, Nana is about to die! But, will I let him die?" At that time, Nana Saheb Chandorkar and Lele Sastri were near Pune. They were in a tonga, the horse of which reared and overturned the tonga. The lives of Nana and Sastri were in peril. But they picked themselves up and found that

> they had suffered no injury. When they reached Shirdi, they found that Baba had made the above declaration and realized He had saved their lives. (*Sri Sai Baba's Charters and Sayings* by Narasimha Swami, p. 229)

Q. What is prostration?

A. Prostration in Hinduism means to stretch out physically, with the face on the ground, in adoration or submission to the Guru, a Ruler, a superior in the family, or even an idol of worship. Prostration is considered to be a physical, symbolic posture of surrender. When a devotee prostrates before the Guru, it indicates self-effacement of his ego and complete faith in the Guru. In some religions, the thought of submission to a superior personality or God is demonstrated by kneeling, kissing of the hand and feet, and bowing down. However, prostration is considered to be the highest form of self-surrender that a Hindu devotee can demonstrate.

Q. Some devotees, when faced with a problem, think that everything must be told to the Guru. Some others are of the view that the Guru being omniscient, automatically comes to know about the problems and give solutions. Therefore, there is no need to tell him everything clearly. What should be the correct approach?

A. According to Shri Sai Satcharita, most of the people who used to meet Baba at Shirdi used to tell him about their major and minor problems and pray for a solution. At times, Shri Sai, the omnipotent Sadguru, used to caution them about the critical and impending problems. However, all Gurus do not possess the power of omniscience to know about the happenings—past, present, and future—of the devotees, without being told about them. Therefore, it is better to tell the Guru about our critical problems and follow his advice.

However, it is not proper to waste the valuable time of the Guru by asking frivolous and repeated questions. In case the Guru chooses to mention about the problems of the devotee to others, it should be taken as the kindness of the Guru to help him. We should not ask questions that are not of a serious or an urgent nature. No devotee should try to usurp the time of the Guru unnecessarily, because his time is meant for other devotees as well. The Sadgurus get very little time for their own comfort because they are always busy, day in and day out, in taking care of their devotees. They try to take rest only after exhausting their entire energy during the day, working for the welfare of the devotees. They render help to devotees located at far off places as well.

> One day Kaka received a letter saying that his younger brother, at Nagpur, was ill. So he said to Baba, "I have received this letter and I am of no service to him." Baba said, "I am of service." Kaka could not make out why Baba said so. But at that very moment, at Nagpur, a sadhu came to attend upon his brother, cured him of his illness, and used the very words of Baba, namely, "I am of service." Kaka, thus, found that even across 1,000 miles, Baba could see what went on and could carry out what was necessary for his *sishya*'s relatives. (Chapter 4, Part II, *Life of Sai Baba* by Narasimha Swami, p. 341)

Q. **What is the meaning of deeksha?**
A. In India, the practice of deeksha or *Guru Deeksha*, is as old as the Guru tradition in Hinduism. It is a spiritual act by which a Guru accepts a spiritual aspirant as his disciple. This practice of acceptance of a disciple by the Guru is prevalent in various religions in different forms. Generally, it is understood to be a preparation or consecration for any spiritual or religious ceremony

The Master and the Disciples

as well. In its substance, deeksha is an unwritten contract between the Guru and the disciple. The disciple agrees to follow the philosophy, ideals, and practices prescribed by the Guru. The Guru agrees to take the responsibility and care for the spiritual training and evolution of the pupil. There is a laid down procedure for deeksha, known as the deeksha ceremony. This also leads to an emotional rapport between the Guru and the disciple.

Spiritual Initiation by Guru
(1 and 2)

The indication (significance) of real deeksha is that it awakens pure devotion. When the dormant bhakti awakens, the disciple turns into a real devotee. The sinful *samskaras* (impressions accumulated from the past lives) get mitigated and virtuous *samskaras* bloom (within him). His personality becomes sanctified. (Volume I, *Shri Guru Bhagavat* English Translation by Shri Chandra Bhanu Satpathy, p. 236)

Initiation in Kaliyug
(55 and 56)

The rules of the game in Kaliyug are different as the bhaktas are illusioned by maya. They come running to the Guru for the fulfilment of their self-interest. They do not have time to pursue the ideals of the Guru. Nor do they have faith, humility, patience or concentration of mind.

(59 and 60)

The Guru imparts knowledge suitable to the capabilities and qualities of the bhakta. Guru does not easily give deeksha to a devotee who is fickle-minded. At first, he imparts lessons on Dharma (righteousness) along with

> social education. The devotee, having put in hard labour, becomes eligible for deeksha. (Volume I, *Shri Guru Bhagavat*, English translation by Shri Chandra Bhanu Satpathy, p. 248)

Q. What is the method of receiving deeksha?

A. Different methods of deeksha daan, that is, the Guru imparting deeksha to the disciple, are practised by different cults or paths of spiritual groups like Vaishnavites, Shaivaites, Saktyas, yogis, tantrics, and others in Hinduism. It becomes a ceremony in which certain prescribed rites or rituals are followed, both by the Guru as well as the disciples, as per the laid down procedure. Usually, the Guru empowers the neophyte spiritually by reciting a mantra (a mystic formula of invocation) in the ears of the disciple. Such spiritual incantation is also performed by the Guru when he touches the body of the disciple or looks deep into his eyes, while reciting the mantra, verbally or mentally, at the same time. When doing so, the Guru infuses in the disciple a stream of divine power, which is necessary to give the disciple a good start. After the initiation, the disciple is supposed to follow the ideals and advice of the Guru and be at his service. This is like an unwritten contract between the Guru and the disciple.

Q. Is it necessary to take deeksha? Did Shirdi Sai Baba give deeksha to His disciples?

A. According to the well-established tradition of Hinduism, deeksha is a sine-qua-non for establishing a spiritual relationship between the Guru and the disciple. In my view, it is a kind of a spiritual discipline and requirement that binds the Master and the disciple together and brings the best out of the disciple. Shirdi Sai Baba does not seem to have given deeksha to any of His devotees in a formal manner, but He has spoken a lot about *atmasakshatkar* or God realization by the devotees.

His methods were unique. He did not follow any of the formal methods of deeksha daan as other Gurus usually practise. Sai Baba was a Sadguru and a mystic of the highest spiritual order. His ways of teaching and evolving the disciples were more subtle and mystique in nature.

He could attract His disciples from far and wide in His own mysterious ways. When the devotee or disciple or anyone He drew to Himself was before Him, He used to spiritually empower him by throwing a glance at him or by speaking a few words with him and even by touching him. Shri Sai Satcharita and the *Sai Leela* magazine are replete with such examples. Some devotees, who visited Shirdi for the first time, became His disciples and remained under His shelter for the rest of their lives. Bala Sahib Bhate's example, as mentioned in Shri Sai Satcharita, highlights this.

Baba has pronounced, "I am not a Guru who whispers mantras in the ears of the disciple." His method of giving spiritual initiation to the devotees was special. Sadgurus, like Shirdi Sai Baba, can establish such spiritual contact or relationship with their devotees even from a distance by the use of their subtle spiritual powers.

Q. **Is deeksha given by other Sadgurus?**
A. Other Sadgurus and Gurus perform the act of deeksha daan in accordance with the paths they follow. For example, Shri Gorakhnath's deeksha method was suited for the practise of Hatha Yoga and Shri Ramakrishna Paramahamsa followed the tantric method of deeksha daan. A study of the autobiographies of the spiritual leaders, saints, and Sadgurus will give an indication about the methods they follow in giving deeksha.

Q. What is the meaning of *samarpana*?

A. In Sanskrit and Hindi, the word *samarpana* means "to surrender". In Hinduism, samarpana has spiritual and religious connotations. In English, the word "surrender" has legal connotations and it means to give up completely into the power of another, for example, the surrender of a prisoner or a criminal to a police authority. In the context of Shri Sai Baba, samarpana implies giving up of oneself emotionally, intellectually, and physically; to be acted upon, guided, and protected by the Master. According to the established Hindu practices, the quality of samarpana to the Sadguru, and through Him to God, is the very basis of spiritual evolution of the pupil.

Q. How can we know that we have really surrendered to Baba?

A. This word *surrender* is easy to utter, but difficult to practice. The word *arpan* in Sanskrit and some other Indian languages means to give away and *samparpana* means to give away completely. In Shri Sai Satcharita, Kaka Saheb Dixit, Megha, and a few other devotees exemplified the essence of this word.

Baba became a Sadguru only after He had completely surrendered to His Guru. We can go through the chapter where Baba has spoken about His experience with His Guru, who tied His legs with a rope and hung him in a well for a few hours. Even in that precarious condition, Baba's faith in His Sadguru did not dwindle.

Once Baba asked the devotees sitting around Him, if anyone could surrender to Him in the manner He had surrendered to His Guru. The devotees had no answer, because they knew that they had not fully surrendered to Baba. A devotee has to wilfully and completely surrender everything of his life to the Guru or God. At the same time, he has to tolerate the adverse experiences of life like worry, doubts, or pain, and that, too, with spontaneous joy. This is called samarpana in the real sense of the term.

> Shama narrated the story of Sai Baba and Radhabai Deshmukh around shraddha and saburi as the cornerstone of a devotee's essential prerequisite for the complete surrender before Guru and God. Baba's teachings to Radhabai were as follows:
>
> "I had a Guru. He was a great Saint and most merciful. I served him long, very long; still he would not blow any mantra into My ears. I had a keen desire, never to leave him but to stay with and serve him; and at all costs receive some instructions from him. But he had his own way. He first got My head shaved and asked Me two pice as dakshina. I gave the same at once. If you ask that as My Guru was perfect, why should he ask for money and how could he be called desire-less, I reply plainly that he never cared for coins. What had he to do with them? His two pice were (1) Firm faith and (2) Patience or perseverance. I gave these two pice or things to him, and he was pleased." (Chapter 18 and 19, *Shri Sai Satcharita*)

Narke's story

As for Baba's declaration about His Guru, Professor Narke heard Baba say, "*Maja Guru* Brahman *ahe*," that is, My Guru is a Brahmin. Having said so much about His Guru, Professor Narke carefully noted that Baba did not say that He had any *sishya* to continue his line. On the other hand, Sai Baba said, "I would tremble to come into the presence of My Guru."

There was no one prepared to serve Sai Baba in that way at Shirdi. Once, Sai Baba asked, it seems, "Who dares to call himself My disciple? Who can serve Me adequately and satisfactorily?" But other than a disciple to continue the line, Baba helped His devotees in various ways and in various degrees. He encouraged them, protected them, and gave them instructions occasionally.

Narke was studying Baba's methods of teaching and improving devotees. Baba gave out moral tales and a few occasional directions. But these were exceptional. But the traditional method of Baba was not oral. His traditional method was, first the negative portion, that is, the Guru did not give to His chosen disciple any Guru mantra. Usually, a Guru whispers a mantra into the ears of the *sishya*, and he seems to be almost biting the ear when he is whispering. So, Baba said, "*Me kanala dasnara* Guru *navhe.*" That is, "I am not the Guru that bites the ear."

He did not regard *japa* and meditation as sufficient for the *sishya*. These produce in the *sadhaka*, *abhimana* or *ahamkara*. Unless and until *ahamkara* is completely wiped out, the Guru is unable to pour all his influence into the *sishya*. In Baba's school, the Guru does not teach. He radiates or pours influence. This influence is poured in and absorbed in full by the soul, which has completely surrendered itself and blotted out the self, but is obstructed by the exercise of intelligence by reliance on self-exertion and by every species of self-consciousness and self-assertion. Baba, therefore, would tell some devotees, "Be by Me and keep quiet and I will do the rest," that is, "secretly or invisibly." Of course, faith in Him—absolute faith—is a prerequisite. A person who was merely seeing Him and staying by Him for a while got faith.

Baba gave experiences, to each devotee, of His vast powers of looking into his heart, into the distant regions

Author doing Pran Pratistha of Shri Shirdi Sai Baba Temple on 20th April, 2014 at Niali, Odisha, India.

On 9th February, 2014, Author doing Pran Prathistha at the Temple at Auckland, New Zealand.

On 12th July, 2014 the Guru Poornima Day, Author dedicating the book Guru Bhagvat (English) Vol-IV to public at Sai Ki Aangan, Gurgoan.

On 19th April 2014, Author receiving Doctorate in Science (DSc) from Shiksha O Anusandhan University, Bhubaneswar, Odisha, India.

Author, as Chief Guest of the 3rd Prarthana Samman Award Function held at Bhubaneswar, organised by Prarthana TV Channel, Odisha.

Author, at the International Release of Shri Sai Satcharita O Shri Sai Aradhana at Dallas, USA.

Author releasing the book at Shri Shirdi Sai Baba's Samadhi Mandir, Shirdi.

On 2nd July, 2014 Author, during pranapratishta of Shri Shirdi Sai Baba Temple at Kochi, Kerala, India.

of space and time, past or future, and thus infused faith. One need not swallow a thing on trust. The solid benefit, temporal or spiritual, reaped by the devotee and his feeling that he is under the eye and power of Baba always, wherever he may be and whatever he may do, gave the devotee an ineradicable basis for his further temporal and spiritual guidance.

Baba's is the Power that controls this world's goods and our fate here and now, as well as our experience and fate in the future, in this world and many unseen worlds. The Professor concludes that the duty of a devotee under Baba is only to keep him fit for the Guru's grace. That is, he should be chaste, pure, simple, and virtuous and he should look trustfully and sincerely to the beloved Master to operate on him secretly, and to raise him to various experiences, higher and higher in range, till he is taken, at last, to the distant goal. "But one step is enough for me," is the proper attitude now. He need not take the trouble to decide complicated metaphysical and philosophical problems about the ultimate destiny. He is ill-prepared to solve them now. The Guru will lift him and endow him with higher powers, vaster knowledge, and increasing realization of truth. And the end is safe in the Guru's hands. (Chapter 8, Part III, *Life of Sai Baba* by B. V. Narasimha Swami, p. 566)

He was studying Yoga Vasishta, a highly philosophical work, which many find very difficult, if not impossible, to understand. About his study of Yoga Vasishta, Baba had something to say, "There are portions even in Yoga Vasishta which would enable one to get into intimate contact with God and be absorbed in Him." When the Professor was reading a passage, apparently of the above sort, Baba told him to give Him 15 rupees dakshina.

> The professor pleaded his impecuniosity saying, "Baba, you know I have no money. Why do you ask me for ₹ 15 dakshina?" Baba said, "Yes, I know it. But you are reading an excellent book now. Get me ₹ 15 dakshina from that." The Professor knew that he should study that special portion of Yoga Vasishta which refers to 15 elements of which one's personality is made up, and present them to Baba in his own heart, as his *antaryami*. That is, he should get *laya* in Baba. (Chapter 8, Part III, *Life of Sai Baba* by B. V. Narasimha Swami, p. 572)

Q. **Does surrender to God lead to the finding of the ultimate truth?**

A. To surrender to God means believing and accepting that God alone is the Sovereign Power of the universe. He is the doer of anything and everything that happens in our life and in the world. Such a surrendered state of mind implies the acceptance of both good and bad events in our life with equanimity. Only a strong belief should exist in us that whatever happens, good or bad, happens in our life because God desires it to be so. This also involves the surrender of our will to the Divine Will of God.

Hence, without asking any questions, we have to accept the truth of life. This is the same as becoming helpless in the face of truth. Such helplessness indicates the destruction of the ego or ahamkara. The basis of devotion to Sai Baba is shraddha and saburi. The ultimate form of shraddha and saburi is to surrender our will to Him. The person who surrenders is helped by Sadguru and God. The person who becomes helpless before Truth, will not feel helpless before any situation or any other person on earth.

10

Shirdi Sai Baba and Sadgurus
(Perfect Masters)

Q. **What is the difference between a Sadguru, a saint and a yogi? Was Shirdi Sai Baba a yogi, saint, or a Sadguru?**

A. It is mentioned in Shri Sai Satcharita that once a devotee saw Baba performing Khand Yoga in Dwarkamayi Masjid. He ran away because he got scared with what he saw. This yogic practice involves separation of various limbs of the body and then re-joining them. Some persons had seen Him performing a yogic practice in Lendi Bagh known as *dhauti*. Once a devotee saw Him taking out His intestines through the mouth, cleaning them, and pushing them back into the stomach.

Baba, as a Sadguru, had mastered the science of yoga. He could control the elements of nature like the fire and rain. He could be seen at more than one place at the same time by different devotees. He had the eighteen siddhi powers under His control. Shri Ramakrishna Paramahamsa had also mastered yogic and tantric practices.

A yogi is a person who is adept in the science of yoga. A saint is a person who is known for piety, holiness, and is considered to be the Chosen One of

God. He may or may not possess siddhi powers. The Sadguru is a saint and also a yogi. But, conversely, all yogis may not be saints. The dominant feature of a Sadguru is His compassion towards all and sundry in the society, as also the pain He takes to help and evolve His disciples. All saints and yogis are necessarily not Sadgurus. A Sadguru is the highest stage of spiritual evolution of any human being on earth.

Baba's Yoga Practices

Baba knew all the processes and practices of yoga. Two of them will be described here:

(1) Dhauti or Cleaning process: Baba went to the well near a Banyan tree, at a considerable distance from the Masjid, every third day and washed his mouth and had a bath. On one occasion, He was seen to vomit out his intestines, clean them inside and outside and place them on a Jamb tree for drying. There are persons in Shirdi who have actually seen this and who have testified to this fact. Ordinary *dhauti* is done by a moistened piece of linen, 3 inches broad, 22 ½ feet long. This piece is gulped down the throat and allowed to remain in the stomach for about half an hour to react with the contents there and then taken out. But Baba's *dhauti* was quite unique and extraordinary.

(2) Khanda Yoga: In this practice, Baba extracted the various limbs from His body and left them separately at different places in the Masjid. Once, a gentleman went to the Masjid and saw Baba's limbs lying separately at separate places. He was very terrified. He first thought of running to the village officers and informing them of Baba being hacked to pieces and murdered. He feared that he would be held responsible, as he was the first informant, and they will presume that he knew

Shirdi Sai Baba and Sadgurus (Perfect Masters) 77

> something of the affair. So he kept silent. But the next day, when he went to the Masjid, he was very surprised to see Baba, hale and hearty, and sound as before. He thought that what he had seen the previous day was only a dream. (Chapter 7, *Shri Sai Satcharita*)

Q. Can a yogi control the elements of nature like water, fire, etc.?

A. Yes, Indian yoga system, propounded by authors like Patanjali and others, hold this theory. Many such examples can be found in Hinduism with reference to saints, yogis, and Sadgurus. In Shri Sai Satcharita (Chapter 11), we can find two such instances — once when Baba controlled the raging fire of the Dhuni and second when he stopped the torrential rain that scared the devotees in Dwarkamayi Masjid.

Patanjali Yoga Shastra mentions about the different siddhi powers that can be acquired through the practice of yoga. Through the use of these powers of siddhi, we can control the elements of nature. The following anecdotes will clarify the point:

> Once, at evening time, there was a terrible storm at Shirdi and rains began to descend in a torrent. In a short time, the whole place was flooded. All the creatures, birds, and people got terribly frightened. They all flocked to the Masjid for shelter. There were many local deities in Shirdi, but none of them came to their help. So they all prayed to Baba. Baba came out and, standing at the edge of the Masjid, addressed the storm in a loud and thunderous voice, "Stop, stop your fury and be calm." In a few minutes, the rain subsided. (Chapter 11, *Shri Sai Satcharita*)
>
> On another occasion, at noon, the fire in the Dhuni began to burn brightly, its flames were seen to be reaching

> the rafters above. Baba soon came to realize what was happening. He took up His *satka* (short stick) and dashed it against a pillar in front, saying, "Get down, be calm." At each stroke of the *satka*, the flames began to lower and slow down and in a few minutes the Dhuni became calm and normal. (Chapter 11, *Shri Sai Satcharita*)

Q. Baba could read the minds of all who came in contact with Him. These persons could be thinking and speaking in different languages. Did Baba know all the languages so that He could read their minds?

A. You have asked an interesting question. Shri Sai Baba and the realized saints possess the siddhi power to read the minds of people, but not necessarily through the medium of the language these people speak. Language is relevant for spoken words and not for the unspoken. The realized saints have the power to penetrate the minds of all living beings through the use of their subtle powers. It is a direct brain to brain communication which does not require the medium of language.

Shirdi Sai Baba was omniscient. He could read the thoughts of His devotees, located even at distant places. Reading the mind of others is one of the siddhi powers that yogis possess.

> Nana Saheb Chandorkar got an order of transfer to Pandharpur and he had to take immediate charge, so he left immediately for Shirdi, without even writing or informing anybody. He wanted to give a surprise visit to Shirdi, see and salute Baba, and then proceed. Nobody even dreamt of Nana Saheb's departure for Shirdi, but Sai Baba knew all about this, as His eyes were everywhere (omniscient). As soon as Nana Saheb approached Neemgaon, a few miles from Shirdi, there was stir in the Masjid at Shirdi. Baba was sitting and talking with Mhalsapati, Appa Shinde, and Kashiram,

> when He suddenly said, "Let us all four do some Bhajan, the doors of Pandhari are open." Then they began to sing in chorus, the main theme of the song being, "I have to go to Pandharpur and I have to stay on there, for it is the house of my Lord." In a short time, Nana Saheb came there with his family, prostrated before Baba, and requested Him to accompany them to Pandharpur and stay with them there. This solicitation was not necessary, as the devotees told Nana Saheb that Baba was already in the mood of going to Pandharpur and staying there. (Chapter 7, *Shri Sai Satcharita*)

Q. How many languages did Baba know? Is there any document, handwritten or signed, by Baba in any language?

A. Baba used to communicate with His devotees generally in Marathi language and local dialects. He knew Urdu and Parsi, as He used to recite *kalmas* from Quran. He knew Hindi, too. His discussion with Nana Saheb Chandorkar pertaining to a *shloka* of Shrimad Bhagavat Gita shows that He knew Sanskrit. I have not come across any information that He communicated through any other language. Some devotees used to send letters, written in Marathi and Hindi, to Baba through Shama, a school teacher and one of His closest devotees. Shama used to elicit answers from Baba and send replies in Marathi on His behalf. It does not seem that Baba ever communicated in writing as no document carrying His handwriting is available.

It is understood that once a judicial magistrate, holding trial of a theft case of Dhule, came to Shirdi to record the statement of Shirdi Sai Baba as a witness in the case. After a lot of persuasion, Baba gave His statement, but did not agree to put His thumb impression or signature to endorse His statement.

When the magistrate asked Him sternly to endorse the document, Baba just made a peculiar sound and went out of Dwarkamayi for begging. The desperate magistrate had no choice but to take help of Kaka Saheb Dixit. However, Baba did not sign any document.

Q. Did Baba deliver spiritual discourses to His devotees on a regular basis? What was His method?

A. Baba never gave lengthy speeches on religious or spiritual themes, as has been the practice with many religious Gurus. Usually, He used to resort to an interactive communication mode with His devotees. Sometimes, He would relate an incident pertaining to the life of a particular devotee who would be sitting amidst the group of devotees, at Dwarkamayi or at Chavadi. During the course of discussion, He would narrate the entire incident, much to the surprise of the concerned devotee. He would spell out the moral of the incident and advise the devotees to do or not do certain things for their spiritual progress. He used to render advice openly and, therefore, all the listeners used to be benefited.

The Sadgurus, usually, render advice when any problem is posed to them or when they anticipate the advent of any problem in the life of a devotee or the community. Unlike the academic world, Baba's way of teaching was most practical, which gave maximum benefit to the largest number of devotees simultaneously. Baba's teachings show an ethical way of existence to the devotees, rather than merely being a philosophical discourse. When replying to the questions put forward by the devotees, Baba, at times, would use parables and anecdotes to bring home the point He wanted to make. At times, His replies would be cryptic, but profound. He did not have a schedule or a calendar for the spiritual training of His devotees.

Besides, Baba used to send many devotees regularly to Sathe Wada and Dixit Wada to listen to the discourses given by Kaka Saheb Dixit, Khaparde, etc., and it is believed that the devotees used to get answers of their queries by listening to these discourses. Therefore, it can be said that Baba had an indirect way of giving answers to the queries of His devotees.

The teachings He imparted were spontaneous and situational in nature. One such anecdote is given below:

Variety in Upadesh — Slanderer Condemned

Sai Baba required no special place, nor any special time for giving instructions. Whenever any occasion demanded, He gave them freely. Once it so happened that a bhakta of Baba reviled another behind his back, before other people. On leaving aside merits, he dwelt on the faults of his brother and spoke so sarcastically that those hearing were disgusted. Generally, we see that people have a tendency for scandalmongering about others unnecessarily and this brings on hatred and ill-will.

Saints see scandal, in another light. They say that there are various ways of cleansing or removing dirt, that is, by means of earth, water, soap, etc., but a scandalmonger has got a way of his own. He removes the dirt (faults) of others by his tongue. So, in a way, he obliges the person whom he reviles and for this he is to be thanked.

Sai Baba had His own method of correcting the scandalmonger. He knew by His omniscience what the slanderer had done and when He met him at noon near Lendi, He pointed out to him a pig that was eating filth near the fence and said to him, "Behold how, with what relish, it is gorging dung. Your conduct is similar. You go on reviling your own brethren to your heart's content.

After performing many deeds of merit, you are born a man, and if you act like this, will Shirdi help you in any way?" Needless to say, the bhakta took the lesson to his heart and went away. (Chapters 18 and 19, *Shri Sai Satcharita*)

Q. Why is the will of a Sadguru said to be the order of God?

A. God alone is the creator of innumerable worlds and the Sadgurus carry on Their divine role on this earth in accordance with the will of God. The unseen divine powers help the Sadgurus in carrying out the will of God. Therefore, every wish of a realized Saint is as potent as an order of God. In other words, everything they will happens, because they don't will anything which is not willed by God. If a Sadguru utters or even thinks of something, the divine powers promptly get activated to fulfil His wishes. Therefore, the blessings and wishes of Sadgurus always come to fructification. The words *Guru Brahma, Gurur Vishnu, Gurur Devo Maheshvarah* simply mean that the Guru or Sadguru possesses the powers of God.

Amra Leela (Mango Miracle)

Damu Anna had three wives. According to his statement, he had not three, but two wives only. He had no issue (child). He consulted many astrologers and himself studied astrology to some extent and found that as there was a *paapi* (inauspicious) planet in his horoscope, there was no prospect of any issue to him in this life. But he had great faith in Baba. One day he received a parcel of mangoes without the name of the sender. When he went to Shirdi, two hours after the receipt of the mango parcel, for worshipping Baba, He said, "Though other people are looking for the mangoes, they are Damu's.

> He whose they are, should eat and die." Damu Anna, on hearing these words, was first shocked. On Mhalsapati explaining to him that death meant the death of the little self or egos, and to have it at Baba's feet was a blessing, he said that he would accept the fruits and eat them. But Baba said to him, "Do not eat yourself, but give them to your junior wife. This Amra Leela (Mango Miracle of 4 mangoes) will give her four sons and four daughters." This was done and ultimately, in due course, it was found Baba's words turned out true and not those of the astrologers. (Chapter 25, *Shri Sai Satcharita*)

Q. **Is it said that Baba used to be pleased more by devotion rather than by the intelligence of the devotees? Is it a disadvantage to be intelligent and an advantage to be unintelligent to receive the grace of Baba?**

A. This concept is correct but your interpretation of the concept is incorrect. The best of the devotees of Baba like Kaka Saheb Dixit, Nana Chandorkar, and many others were extremely intelligent persons who were highly placed in life before they came to Baba. Shri Kaka Saheb Dixit was a famous solicitor of Mumbai and Nana Saheb Chandorkar was a First Class Magistrate of the British Government. They were extremely intelligent and had full faith in Baba. Shri Vivekananda, the most prominent disciple of Shri Ramakrishna Paramahamsa, was a brilliant man.

Such persons utilized their intelligence in accordance with the ideals of the Sadguru whom they followed. These devotees had complete knowledge about worldly affairs. Yet, they had the right type of intelligence to understand the greatness of the Guru and His divine role. Therefore, they sacrificed their worldly comforts and blindly followed the Sadguru. Their emotional link with the Sadguru and their devotion was exemplary. Being both devotional and intelligent at the same time, they could do a lot to spread the glory of Shirdi Sai Baba effectively. Lack of intelligence, as much as misuse of intelligence, is not a virtue. Proper use of intelligence helps a person to evolve, both in the material world as well as in the spiritual world.

Q. Some devotees used to address Shirdi Sai Baba as *Sai Mauli*. What is its significance?

A. When He was at Shirdi, in the initial stage, the majority of the devotees who used to visit Sai Baba were Maharashtrians. In Marathi language, the word *mauli* means mother.

The Sadgurus take care of all the needs of Their devotees compassionately and with a lot of pain and effort, because they love them immensely, like Their own children. They pardon the mistakes of the devotees countless number of times. These are the basic qualities of a mother. Shri Shirdi Sai Baba used to protect and support His devotees, day in and day out. He used to save them from all sorts of dangers, seen and unseen. He used to teach them the way of an ethical existence, as a mother does to her children. Like a mother, teaching the basic alphabets of language to the infant, the Sadguru taught the basic principles of evolution to the neophytes. Numerous examples of such acts of kindness of Baba towards His devotees can be found in Shri Sai Satcharita. That is why, at times, they used to address Him as mother.

Shirdi Sai Baba used to refer to the Dwarkamayi Masjid, at Shirdi, as His mother.

Even in the Night Aarti which used to be sung earlier by the devotees, the word *Mauli* is used to address Baba.

Ovalu arati majhya sadgurunatha, majha Sainatha
Panchahi tatvancha deep lavila ata
Nirgunanchi sthiti kaisee aakara ali
Sarvaghati bharuni urli Sai Mauli
Ovalu

Balasaheb Mirikar

This is our Dwarkamayi, where you are sitting. She wards off all dangers and anxieties of the children, who sit on her lap. This Masjidmayi (its presiding Deity) is very merciful; she is the mother of the simple devotees, whom she will save in calamities. Once a person sits on her lap, all his troubles are over. He, who rests in her shade, gets bliss. (Chapter 22, *Shri Sai Satcharita*)

Mrs Radhabai Deshmukh

"My Guru never expected any other thing from Me. He never neglected Me, but protected Me at all times. I lived with Him and was sometimes away from Him; still I never felt the want or absence of His love. He always protected Me by His glance, just as the tortoise feeds her young ones, whether they are near her or away from her on the other side of the river bank, by her loving looks. Oh mother, My Guru never taught Me any mantra, then how shall I blow any mantra in your ears? Just remember that Guru's tortoise-like loving glance gives us happiness. Do not try to get mantra or upadesh from anybody. Make Me the sole object of your thoughts and actions; and you will, no doubt, attain Paramartha (the spiritual goal of life). Look at Me wholeheartedly, and I in turn will look at you similarly. Sitting in this Masjid, I speak the truth, nothing but the truth. No sadhanas, nor proficiency in the six Shastras, are necessary. Have faith and confidence in your Guru. Believe fully, that Guru is the sole Actor or Doer. Blessed is he who knows the greatness of his Guru and thinks him to be Hari, Hara, and Brahma (Trimurti) Incarnate." Instructed in this way, the old lady (Radhabai) was convinced; she bowed to Baba and gave up her fast.

"The (mother) tortoise is on one bank of the river, and her young ones are on the other side. She gives neither milk, nor warmth to them. Her mere glance gives them nutrition. The young ones do nothing, but remember (meditate upon) their mother. The tortoise glance is, to the young ones, a downpour of nectar, the only source of sustenance and happiness. Similar is the relation between the Guru and disciples." (Chapter 18 and 19, *Shri Sai Satcharita*)

Q. Baba used to make jokes with His devotees even when dealing with serious matters or replying to serious questions. Why did He do so?

A. Sadgurus like Baba and Shri Ramakrishna Paramahamsa used to joke and have a lot of fun with the devotees. Their answers to the most serious questions often used to be humorous. Humour is an excellent way of teaching the disciples. At times, when a devotee would approach Baba to elicit an answer of an important question or to seek solution of a difficult problem, he would do so with extreme care. A student can ask a question with clarity only when he is at ease to communicate with the mentor. Baba used to resort to humour and jocularity to make the devotee feel confident before asking the question. At times, He used to diffuse an unpleasant or a serious situation arising between devotees by tempering down the unwarranted seriousness of the issue through humour. He used to explain the highest principles of ethics and philosophy using the simplest form of language for easy understanding of the devotees. The story of channa (gram) mentioned in Shri Sai Satcharita, Chapter 24, is one such example.

Chanak Leela

In Shirdi, bazaar was held every Sunday and people from the neighbouring villages came there, erected booths and stalls on the street, and sold their wares and commodities. Every noon, the Masjid was crowded, more or less; but on Sunday, it was crowded to suffocation. On one such Sunday, Hemadpant sat in front of Baba, shampooing His legs and reciting God's name. Shama was on Baba's left, Vamanrao to His right. Shriman Buti, Kaka Saheb Dixit, and others were also present there. Then, Shama laughed and said to Anna Saheb (Hemadpant), "See, some grains seem to have stuck to the sleeve of your coat." So saying, he touched the sleeve and found that there were some grains. Hemadpant straightened his left forearm to see what the matter was, when to the surprise of all, some grains of gram came rolling down and were picked up by the people who were sitting there.

This incident furnished the subject-matter for some jokes. Everybody present began to wonder and said something or other as to how the grains found their way into the sleeve of the coat and lodged there so long. Hemadpant also could not guess how they found a place and stayed there. When nobody could give any satisfactory explanation of this matter, and everybody was wondering about this mystery, Baba had the following conversation:

Baba: This fellow (Anna Saheb) has got the bad habit of eating alone. Today is a bazaar day and he was there munching grams. I know his habit and these grams are a proof of it. What wonder is there in this matter?

Hemadpant: Baba, I never know of eating things alone; then why do you thrust this bad habit on me? I have not yet seen Shirdi bazaar today. I never went to the bazaar today, then how could I buy grams, and how could I eat them if I had not bought them? I never eat anything unless I share it with others present near me.

Baba: It is true that you give to the persons present; but if none be nearby, what could you or I do? But do you remember Me before eating? Am I not always with you? Then, do you offer Me anything before you eat?

Moral

Let us mark and note carefully what Baba has taught us by this incident. To put the matter in a nutshell, we should not enjoy any object with our senses, etc., without first remembering our Guru. When the mind is trained in this way, we will always be reminded of Baba, and our meditation on Baba will grow quickly. The *sagun* form of Baba will ever be before our eyes and then devotion, non-attachment, and salvation will all be ours. When Baba's form is thus fixed before our mental vision, we forget hunger, thirst, and this *samsar*; the consciousness of worldly pleasures will disappear and our mind shall attain peace and happiness. (Chapter 24, *Shri Sai Satcharita*)

Anna Chinchanikar

There is a mention about two devotees named Damodar Ghanashyama Babare and Venubai Koujalgi who created an unpleasant situation in Dwarkamayi when meeting Baba.

One day, a devotee by the name Damodar Ghanashyama Babare, alias Anna Chinchanikar, was shampooing the

> left arm of Baba, which rested on the railing. On the right side, one old widow named Venubai Koujalgi, whom Baba called mother and all others called her Mavsibai, was serving Baba in her own way. This Mavsibai was an elderly woman of pure heart. She was kneading Baba's abdomen. She did this so forcefully that Baba's back and abdomen became flat (one). While doing so, Mavsibai's face moved up and down with her strokes and once came very close to the face of Anna. She remarked, "Oh, this Anna is a lewd (bad) fellow, he wants to kiss me. Even being so old with grey hair, he feels no shame in kissing me." These words enraged Anna and he replied back, "You say that I am an old, bad fellow, am I quite a fool? It is you that have picked up a quarrel and are quarrelling with me." All the persons present there were enjoying this encounter. Baba, who loved both of them, said, "Oh Anna, why are you unnecessarily raising this hue and cry? I do not understand what harm or impropriety is there when the mother is kissed!" Baba's humorous words immediately diffused the situation. (Chapter 24, *Shri Sai Satcharita*)

Q. **It is said that the freedom fighters of the Indian national movement used to visit Baba. What was His advice to them?**

A. Yes, that was the time when resentment against the British rule by the native Indians had started increasing. Many prominent freedom fighters of that time used to visit Baba. If we go through the history of India's freedom struggle, we will come to know that, in 1907, Indian National Congress was divided in two groups about the method of fighting for freedom. The revolutionary group was lead by Shri Bal Gangadhar Tilak and the moderate group was led by Shri Gopal Krishna Gokhale. Lala Lajpat Rai was busy with organizing protests in Punjab. It is well known that Bal Gangadhar Tilak came to Baba on the May 19, 1917, with his closest associate, G. S. Khaparde, a prominent lawyer and solicitor of Amravati.

G. S. Khaparde, on his visits to Shirdi, used to spend long periods of time with Baba. Kaka Saheb Dixit belonged to the moderate group. He was so attached to Baba that he left all the material aspects of his life, built a Wada in Shirdi, and fully served Baba till the end of his life.

Besides these prominent personalities, other freedom fighters also used to visit Him for gaining spiritual strength and solace. The British Government, through its spies, used to keep a close watch on the happenings around Baba. Baba used to address these police officers, wearing plain clothes, as "Govindas".

When Bal Gangadhar Tilak met Baba, Baba asked him to take rest as he had done enough and also advised him not to reveal his secrets to anyone. Shri Sai was a Sadguru, who laboured day-in and day-out for the evolution of his devotees. There is no record, not even in Khaparde's diary, to indicate that Baba ever gave advice on political issues.

> On May 19, 1917, the political leader, Bal Gangadhar Tilak, paid a visit to Sai Baba, along with G. S. Khaparde. As per Khaparde's diary, "We went to the Masjid and paid our respects to Sai Maharaj. I never saw him so pleased before.... Looking at Lokmanya He said, 'People are bad, keep yourself to yourself.'"
> Sai Baba also said to Lokamanya, "You have done much for the people, but now you should also take care of your soul." Within three years thereof, Lokamanya died. (*The Life and Teachings of Sai Baba of Shirdi* by Rigopoulos, pp. 227–228 and pp. 300–301, *Sai Sharan Anand Shri Sai Baba*, Translated by V.B. Kher, pp. 300–301)

Shirdi Sai Baba and Sadgurus (Perfect Masters)

Q. **Baba used to refer to the police spies as "Govindas". What was the view of the British government about Shri Sai?**

A. Available intelligence reports of the British government show that the police spies and detectives of the Criminal Investigation Department (C.I.D.) used to report that Baba was a saintly person, whom both Hindus and Muslims respected. The reason for the visit of prominent leaders; Indian officials of the British Raj like magistrates, revenue and police officials; and other prominent personalities used to perplex the British intelligence agencies. They presumed that prominent personalities used to visit Him to know about the future of the British rule in India and also to extract oracles from Shri Sai Baba regarding the fall of the British rule, which they could then use to spread disaffection against the British government. Such speculations were baseless. Baba never gave advice on political issues.

The police spies used to position themselves around Baba inside Dwarkamayi Masjid, where Baba used to stay. They kept a watch on all the devotees, particularly government officials and other prominent personalities who used to frequent Baba. Everything Baba said to important persons used to be recorded by the spies in their official diaries and forwarded to C.I.D. high-ups.

Q. **British government officials like Nana Saheb Chandorkar, Rao Bahadur Sathe, Justice Rege, and many others used to visit Baba frequently. Were they not afraid of visiting Shri Sai, who was under intelligence surveillance of the British government?**

A. As officials of the British government, they would have surely been aware that the police spies would be keeping a watch on them when they visited Baba. However, they were so intensely attached to Baba and had so much faith in Him that they never seemed to be afraid of the probable official consequences of their frequent visits to Shirdi. They were convinced that nothing could go wrong when they were under the protection of their Sadguru. Whenever they were in trouble, they found that Shri Sai helped them out of the difficult situation in the most unexpected manner. There is no history of any devotee suffering at the hands of their employer or the Government because of his visit to Baba or for the unauthorized absence from duty.

On the other hand, by following the instructions of Baba, some devotees benefited even in court cases. Some of these devotees gave a priority to Baba's orders over the orders of their superior officers of the department. However, they never suffered.

> Nana was staying with Baba at Shirdi and wanted to start one morning to go to Kopergaon, where he had an appointment to meet the Collector. When he went to take leave of Baba at the proper time, Baba simply said, "Go tomorrow". Nana had full faith in Baba, took leave of Baba the next day. Baba then said, "You now go and meet the Collector." When Nana went to Kopergaon and enquired of the office staff there as to what happened the previous day, they said that the Collector had sent a telegram that he was not coming that day, but only on the following day. Baba did not receive a copy of the telegram, but by his own *antarjnana* knew of the postponement of the appointment and gave Nana the benefit of it with the resulting further benefit of an extra day's stay with his Guru. Thus, even in the most important official matters, Nana's faith made him follow Baba's words with great advantage to himself, temporally and spiritually. (Chapter 2, Part II, *Life of Sai Baba* by Narasimha Swami, p. 261)

> H. S. Dixit was the sole living witness to a will he drew up and when that will came up for probate in the Mumbai High Court, he had necessarily to be summoned. The summons were served at Shirdi and Dixit was legally bound to appear in Court at Mumbai as a witness and the party's agent came to Shirdi to take him. But Baba did not give him permission to start. This looked awkward—nay risky. But at Mumbai, the case was adjourned that day to another date. Even for the subsequent postings, Dixit was not allowed to start. Baba knew that the hearing would not take place. The citing party got vexed and was considering if the only remaining course, that is, the issue of warrant to secure Dixit's presence, should be adopted. He wired to Dixit. This time, Baba sent Dixit and he was examined in Court. Baba knew exactly at what point he should stop detention. (Chapter 4, Part II, *Life of Sai Baba* by Narasimha Swami, p. 354)

Q. Did any officer of British nationality ever visit Shri Sai Baba at Shirdi?

A. Many British officials like the Revenue Commissioner Mr Curtis, Collector of Ahmednagar and the Assistant Collector are reported to have visited Baba during their official tour to the area. Some of them used to visit Him out of curiosity and for the direct verification of facts as Baba used to be admired by all. Only a few came to Him to take His blessings. The Commissioner, Mr Curtis, had come to Shirdi with his wife, who wanted to take the blessings of Baba to have a child. Baba did not meet him or oblige them because Mr Curtis was an arrogant person who tried to dictate his terms to Baba.

British officials like the Sub Inspector of Schools, who used to come on inspection of the local school (in which Shama was employed), used to visit Baba, too. Many more British officials would have met Him because Baba stayed at Shirdi for over five decades.

Baba became angry one day and said, at Dwarkamayi, "Rascal! Coming to see me! What have I got? I am a naked fakir with human organs." People could not make out whom Baba was referring to. But soon the full official procession, headed by Mrs and Mr Curtis and followed by the Collector, the Assistant Commissioner, and others, passed in front of the Dwarkamayi. Then they went on to the Chavadi and from there wished to send word to Baba. That was, however, impossible as no one would convey orders to Baba. Then Baba himself passed in front of the Chavadi and Mrs Curtis wished to have a talk. Baba said, "Wait for half an hour." But Baba returned within ten minutes and she again said she wished to have a talk. Baba said, "Wait for one hour." The officers were impatient. Mr Curtis was done with Baba and Shirdi and they went off. Of course, Mrs Curtis's object, namely, to get a child by Baba's blessings, was not achieved. (Chapter 8, Part III, *Life of Sai Baba* by Narasimha Swami, p. 570)

European Gentleman

One European gentleman of Mumbai once came to Shirdi with an introductory note from Nana Saheb Chandorkar and with some object in view. He was comfortably accommodated in a tent. He wanted to kneel before Baba and kiss His hand. Therefore, he tried thrice to step into the Masjid, but Baba prevented him from doing so. He was asked to sit in the open courtyard below and take Baba's darshan from there. Not pleased with this reception he got, he wanted to leave Shirdi at once and came to bid goodbye. Baba asked him to go the next day and not to hurry. People also requested him to abide by Baba's directions. Not listening to all this, he left Shirdi

> in a tonga. The horses ran all right at first, but when Sawul well was passed, a bicycle came in front, seeing which the horses were frightened and ran fast. The tonga was turned topsy-turvy and the gentleman fell and was dragged some distance. He was immediately released from the tonga but had to go and remain in Kopergaon hospital for the treatment of his injuries. Because of such experiences, all people learnt the lesson that those who disobeyed Baba's instructions met with accidents in one way or the other, and those who obeyed them were safe and happy. (Chapter 9, *Shri Sai Satcharita*)

Q. There is a mention of the magazine *Sainath Prabha* in Shri Sai Satcharita. Please tell us something about it.

A. Shri Sai Satcharita mentions briefly about a magazine titled *Sainath Prabha*. This magazine was bilingual (Marathi and English). It was published by the Dakshina Bhiksha Sansthan and a prominent devotee of Baba called Rao Bahadur H. V. Sathe. It was printed in Pune and published from Shirdi. The importance of this magazine lies in the fact that it brings out the actual happenings in Shirdi related to Shri Sai Baba's activities and sayings. The articles contained in the magazine can be used as a primary evidence by the researchers on Baba (Chapter 2, *Shri Sai Satcharita*).

Q. Was there any devotee who could come up to the expectations of Sai Baba?

A. Many devotees used to come to Baba only for their spiritual evolution, but in very few numbers. People who used to come to Shirdi for spiritual evolution always stayed near Baba, meditated on and worshipped Him and tried to serve Him. They had unshakable faith in Baba. While living in Shirdi they used to spend most of their time in meditation and for reading of religious scriptures, besides serving Baba. They used to listen carefully to whatever Baba had to say. They always tried to comprehend the true meaning of His sayings and implement the instructions of Baba in their lives. They always remained alert and were anxious to follow the orders of Baba, both in letter and spirit. Their only prayer to Baba was to purify their hearts, reduce their worldly attachments and enable their advancement in the path of salvation. These devotees used to get complete protection from Baba. Baba used to remain awake even during nights to protect the devotees, whether they were near or far away from Him. In this manner, some prominent devotees were able to come up to the expectations of Baba.

> At college, Balasaheb Bhate was a free thinker, a free smoker, a veritable *Charvaka* whose creed may be thus summed up: "Eat, drink, and be merry today, for tomorrow we die." I used to remark jocularly at his inveterate smoking, being myself free of the tobacco habit. He became a Mamlatdar and was a very efficient officer, much liked by his Collector. He was the Mamlatdar of Kopergaon for about five years (1904-1909). All that time he was scoffing at his educated friends (who met him on their way to Shirdi), not having any respect for Sai, whom he described as "a mad man". His friends asked him to see Sai Baba just once and then form his judgement. In 1909, Bhate camped at Shirdi and saw Sai Baba, day after day. On the fifth day, Sai Baba covered him with a *gerua* (earthy-red colour) garment. From that day, Bhate was a changed man. He did not care for earnings or work. From that day, up to his death, he only wished to be at Shirdi, to do *seva* to Sai Baba, to live and die in His presence. Sai Baba made his friend Dixit draw up an application for leave for one year and with His help, Bhate's signature was taken on it. The Collector gave him one year's time

> to see if he would return to his old self. But, at the end of the year, he still continued to be "mad after his Guru" and was granted compassionate pension of about 30 rupees, as one afflicted with "religious melancholia".
>
> Asked for the reason of his change, Bhate told me the putting of the (*bhagawa*) *gerua* garment on him by Sai Baba marked the turning point. "By that," he said, "my original frame of mind was removed and in its place quite a new frame of mind was put in." After that, attending to worldly duties — especially official duties — became unthinkable. He then lived at Shirdi, attending to his Nitya Karma, Upanishad reading, etc., before Sai (Sai would offer remarks on that reading occasionally). His wife and family came to Shirdi and lived with him. (Chapter 4, Part III, *Devotees' Experiences of Sri Sai Baba* by Narasimha Swami)

Q. Does an ordinary human being become a Sadguru or does a special power descends from heavens in the form of the Sadguru?

A. According to the principle of evolution or *vivartanvaad*, life forms evolved on our globe from the stage of fish, tortoise, and animals to that of the human race. Intelligence or *manas tattwa* has the highest development in human beings compared to any other species. Through many births, the human race has evolved its *manas tattwa* or intelligence to such heights that it has got superior knowledge and competence to control the various powers of nature. The most evolved human beings reach the state of *shivatama* from the state of *jeevatama*. For a person who is a shivatama, his actions are not for his own cause or for the cause of his family alone, but he becomes capable of giving evolution to all the living beings and species on earth. Such evolved souls, who have the capability to control the forces of nature and use them for the good of others, are known as *Sadguru*. A person becomes a Sadguru only when he reaches the stage of a shivatama. However, during the destabilization of the social order or Dharma on the earth, divine powers like Shri Rama and Shri Krishna incarnate on earth, in a human body. Incarnation means the advent on earth of a divine power in a human body.

Q. Why is it that when someone gets connected to a Sadguru, his relatives and friends also generally get drawn towards Him?

A. The greater the purity in thought, emotion, and devotion of a devotee, the stronger is the influence of the Sadguru on the devotee and also on his relatives and friends. For instance, when an electric bulb is switched on, the light gives benefit to all within its ambit or sphere of influence. In the same way, when an individual gets connected with a Sadguru, the spiritual impact slowly permeates the consciousness of other family members and all the persons who are close to him. In other words, Guru Shakti gets transmitted through the devotee to his relatives and friends. The devotee only becomes a medium for the power belongs to the Sadguru. Shri Sai Satcharita mentions that many non-devotees got drawn to Baba through the medium of ardent devotees. A devotee named Nana Saheb Chandorkar became Baba's medium to bring hundreds of other devotees to Shirdi. Similarly, Dasganu Maharaj, a famous *kirtankar* inspired many people to visit Baba. It is said that anyone who visited Baba even once, became His devotee.

Nana Saheb Chandorkar was instrumental in bringing to Shirdi several great devotees like Dixit, Dabholkar, Dasganu, Radhakrishna Mai, Moreshwar Pradhan, Tatyasaheb Noolkar, Balasaheb Deo, Madhavrao Adkar, Vinayakrao Thakur, Kashibai Cankered, Chintamanrao Vaidya and others. Rao Bahadur S. B. Dhumal was instrumental in getting Gopal Rao Buti to Shirdi.

Radhakrishna Ayi was anxious to direct society's important people to Baba's feet, and wanted to get P. R. Avaste, a retired Judge of Gwalior, to Baba's feet. So, Rege tried to bring him over to Shirdi. Baba, on the silent prayer of Rege, helped Avaste to get over the obstacles. The main objection Avaste had was that he already had another Guru, a lady with a remarkable personality and powers and going to see Baba would be *gurudroha* towards her. Then, Rege told him that Sai Baba was the same spirit as the spirit in all Gurus and, therefore, in that lady also and he might therefore go to Shirdi and feel that the lady was in Baba. Avaste agreed to go during Christmas of 1914. But there was a great obstacle. Avaste was very slow and allowed arrears of work to accumulate. He then sat up and in the first few days of the holidays cleared off the work, much to his own surprise. This was the evidence of Baba's help.

When they started, there was another and very unexpected obstacle. It was war time in 1914 and trains were being requisitioned. Going from Indore to Manmad, at Mhow, a Cantonment station, their train was commandeered. All passengers were asked to get down. Just as they were about to get down, the Commanding Officer came up and asked them to stay on, as their particular compartment was not going to be taken by the military, because it was too small and unnecessary. Obviously, it was Baba's work and Baba said so when they reached Shirdi. Then, when they were in the train, Rege went on all night with his chantings and bhajans, calling on Baba. When they reached Shirdi, Baba asked Rege, "Who is this *pissat*, the crazy man with you?" This proved to be a prophecy. Again, Baba went on referring to Rege, saying, "Look at him. He will not be content to come alone. He insists on others being brought." This again had reference to Rege's desire not to start until and unless Avaste also started with him. Again, Baba said, "They wanted to put My children out of the train. But I told the Commanding Officer, they are My children, let them come to Me." This indicated how they were allowed to travel by that train as an exception. Lastly, Baba said, "He gave Me no sleep, last night. All night, Baba, Baba, was the cry around My bedside." These four references showed that Baba was watching His children and using all His powers to influence all minds to favour their pious endeavours to be with Him and profit thereby. (Chapter 5, Part III, *Life of Sai Baba* by Narasimha Swami, p. 532)

Q. Baba has said that He draws His devotee towards Him just like pulling a bird whose legs are tied with a thread. How does this happen?

A. Shri Sai Satcharita tells us that Baba used to attract many of His devotees to Shirdi, in some way or the other. Kaka Saheb Dixit, Nana Saheb Chandorkar, Upasani Baba, and Dasganu Maharaj are but a few examples. A Sadguru knows the past and present of all the devotees and draws them by His divine powers. Confused by maya or ignorance, some devotees try to resist the mighty divine pull but, ultimately, come to the Spiritual Master. The Sadguru draws the devotee to Him only when He considers it appropriate to do so. A person cannot force his way to the Sadguru without His wishes.

Shri Narayan Govind Chandorkar was the Personal Assistant to the Collector of Ahmednagar and was camping at Kopergaon for *jamabandi*, that is, land revenue settlement work. All *karnams* of the *taluk* had to attend at the *jamabandi* and the Shirdi *karnam* also had to attend. The Shirdi *karnam*, Appa Kulkarni, went to Baba and asked Him leave to go to Kopergaon for *jamabandi* work, as the Personal Assistant to the Collector, Narayan Govind Chandorkar, was there. Baba gave him leave and added, "Tell your Nana to come here."

With great diffidence, the *karnam*, at the close of the day, approached the Deputy Collector and told him that Sai Baba, a fakir of Shirdi, had invited him to come to Shirdi. Chandorkar was astounded. He thought that it could not possibly be, and told the *karnam* that he was a stranger to the fakir and the fakir was a stranger to him, and that he, the *karnam*, must have some purpose of his own to invite him to his village. In spite of the *karnam's* protests, Chandorkar would not believe him and sent him away.

When the *karnam* reported his failure to Baba, Baba repeated the invitation, and again the *karnam*, with considerable diffidence, approached the Deputy Collector the second day and repeated the invitation. The second invitation had the same fate for the same reasons as the first. That again was reported to Baba. Baba pressed the hesitating *karnam* to repeat the invitation for the third time. Nana Chandorkar thought that there must be something in it and so he told the *karnam* that he would visit Shirdi, but not immediately. Chandorkar, after going to Ahmednagar, did go and pay a visit to Shirdi. After meeting Baba, Nana Saheb Chandorkar started serving Baba for the rest of his life. (Chapter 2, Part II, *Life of Sai Baba* by Narasimha Swami)

Kashinath Upasani Baba came to Rahuri where a yogi (Kulkarni) advised him to go to Sai Baba, but he declined to go to a Mohammedan and went to Jejuri and then to Kedgaonbet (to Narayan Maharaj). Shri Upasani's first Shirdi visit was on June 27, 1911. After staying at Shirdi for about two or three days, he wanted to leave for home.

> Sai did not agree. When Kashinath pleaded vehemently, Sai Baba permitted him on the condition that he should return to Shirdi in eight days. Kashinath started worrying and Sai Baba told him, "Well, go if you like, I will see what I can do."
>
> Moving from place to place, Kashinath reached Kopergaon, eight miles away from Shirdi, on the eighth day and was utterly confused. He came back to Shirdi and met Shri Sai again. Baba said to Kashinath, "You have come back! How many days is it since you left?" "This is the eighth day," confessed Kashinath. "What!" Baba remarked, "You said you would not come back in eight days." Then the spell over Kashinath seemed to disappear and he woke up and said, "What, Baba, I cannot understand this. I was eager to go home, and I wonder how I did not go back home. This must be all your doing." Baba said, "Yes. I have been with you all these eight days, dogging your heels." (Chapter 2, Part II, *Life of Sai Baba* by Narasimha Swami)

Q. It is mentioned that Baba neither slept nor allowed Mhalsapati and Tatya Kote Patil to go to sleep for years, when they used to spend nights together at Dwarkamayi Masjid. Is it possible for the Sadgurus to go without sleep?

A. The Sadgurus are adept in the science of yoga. They don't sleep like an ordinary human being, who loses his consciousness in the state of sleep and sees dreams. The Sadgurus enter into a state of yogic sleep. In this state, they appear to be sleeping but they don't lose their consciousness. The physical body rests but the consciousness is not withdrawn. This is how Baba used to take rest at night. Because He was ever wakeful and, therefore, He could wake up the other two when they used to fall asleep.

The Sadgurus are fully capable of controlling their consciousness. It is understood that the Sadgurus visit different places and also their devotees at night to solve their problems even while pretending to be asleep.

Baba, at night, had to watch people, for night is chiefly the time of danger. The Nigoj village Munsif was a bhakta of Baba. Plague raged in Nigoj. The village Munsif's wife was attacked and was in imminent peril of death from plague. At that time, Baba, in the Mosque, told Mhalsapati, "Come, today we shall have a special watch. You know what takes place in Nigoj? The rude Rohilla (plague) wants to kill the Patil's wife. But I am praying to Allah to save her. So you better see that nobody comes and disturbs my prayer." So Baba went on intensely concentrating on His loving task of saving that lady. But fate willed it otherwise. The Mamlatdar's peon broke into the Mosque at that time and wanting Baba's Udi, disturbed Baba's concentration and then the result was that the concentrated prayers stopped. Baba at once saw with His wonderful vision that the lady died. So He got angry with Mhalsapati for having allowed the interference and then finally added, "The lady is dead. What has happened is for good."

This is a very striking instance of how Baba spent His nights. As Baba said, His nights were not intended for sleep. On the other hand, with His divine eye of supervision, He was keeping a watch over all His bhaktas in all their places and averting danger for them." (Chapter 1, Part III, *Life of Sai Baba* by Narasimha Swami, p. 492)

Night and day, I think and think of my people, I call their names over and over again. To S. B. Dhumal He said, "*Bhau*, the whole of last night, I had no sleep. I lay thinking and thinking of you. At every step I have to take care of you, else what will happen to you, God knows." (*Sri Sai Baba's Charters and Sayings* by Narasimha Swami, p. 6)

Q. We have heard that when Baba was in Shirdi, He never used to sleep and kept reciting *Hari Naam* throughout the night. Is this true?

A. Shri Shirdi Sai Baba was not only a Sadguru, but also a *Jeevan Mukta*. Whether a *Jeevan Mukta* chooses to be in His body or chooses to leave His body, He always remains in a state of complete consciousness. Even when a Sadguru performs any physical actions through the medium of His body, He simultaneously remains active in the subtle body as well. It can be said that these divine souls take a human form or use the body as a cover for the soul in the same way as we cover ourselves with a blanket. When the preordained divine role gets completed, they leave the body at will, in the same way as ordinary mortals remove their clothes from their body. Therefore, they are not in the need of food or sleep as other human beings. Their physical body remains fit even without food. Many saints are reported to have remained without food for several years. Even when lying in a sleeping posture, they remain in a complete wakeful state.

> Baba would tell Mhalsapati, "You had better sit up. Do not go to sleep. Place your hand on my heart. I will be going on with remembrance of Allah *Nama Smaran*, that is, a half conscious trance, and during that *Nama Smaran*, the heartbeat would clearly show you that I am still having *Nama Smaran*. If that suddenly goes away and natural sleep supervenes, wake me up." The heartbeat during natural sleep would be evidently different from the heart beat of the contemplative trance. Thus, neither Baba nor Mhalsapati would sleep at night. (Chapter 1, Part II, *Life of Sai Baba* by Narasimha Swami, p. 225)

Shirdi Sai Baba and Sadgurus (Perfect Masters)

Q. Did Shirdi have any special significance for Baba to settle down?

A. No one can answer this question with exactitude except the Master Himself. On the basis of the information that is available, I can only attempt to give an answer. It is a well-known fact that Baba came to Shirdi for the first time with the marriage party of Chandbhai Patel from Dhoopkheda village. Maybe if He had not accompanied this marriage party or if the marriage had been fixed in some other village, He would not have come to Shirdi at all. This is a rational way of looking at things.

Shri Sai Satcharita mentions about the existence of a small underground cellar near the neem tree located in the Gurusthan which was accidentally discovered by the villagers when digging earth. Baba is reported to have said that His Guru used to practise meditation in a "4x4x4" cellar for twelve years. The cellar had four lamps burning in it and its entrance was closed by a quern stone. The cell was paved with limestone and contained a wooden seat, a Gomukhi with a beautiful rosary. The cellar was closed by the villagers at His behest. This means that Baba had knowledge about it before coming to Shirdi.

There exists another reference which connects one of His earlier births with Shirdi. The Sadguru could have decided to perform His divine activities from Shirdi taking into consideration these and many other factors which remain unknown to us.

A similar story has also been reported in *Sai Leela* magazine which is excerpted below:

> Gurusthan—This is My father's place. One day Baba told that at this place there is a *turbat* (*mazaar*) of a *peer*. When it was excavated, a *turbat* was found there. That day, villagers took Baba in a procession, playing musical instruments. Baba told Kaka Saheb

that this is My father's place and asked him to light perfumed sticks on every Thursday and Friday and he will be benefited. (*Sai Leela*, 1923, Ank 1)

Q. It is mentioned in Shri Sai Satcharita that when Baba first came Shirdi, He used to spend some time in a Takia, where He used to sing and dance. Where is the Takia in Shirdi?

A. The Takia building has been demolished since long and the land has been utilized for new construction. A new but small building, which is situated on the northern side of the Samadhi Mandir, is being used by the management for public relations purposes. Many buildings, including the school where Shama, one of the closest devotees of Baba, used to teach, have been demolished. Many places and buildings mentioned in Shri Sai Satcharita have been altered. After 2018, a century would have passed since the Mahaprayan of Baba in 1918.

Q. Baba's closest devotee, Shama, used to teach in a school which was in close proximity of Dwarkamayi Masjid. Can you please tell me its location as I could not find it?

A. I am sorry to say that the school was demolished a few years ago. In its place a big commercial complex has been constructed. The school was located on the north side of Dwarkamayi and on the western side of the old Hanuman temple (slightly behind it). I had visited the school before demolition and had photographed it.

It had a row of rooms stretching from East to West and a playground. From one of the windows of the school, Dwarkamayi was visible. Shama is reported to have kept a constant watch on Baba through this window when Baba first settled at Dwarkamayi Masjid. At the time of Baba, Dwarkamayi had a mud wall of

Shirdi Sai Baba and Sadgurus (Perfect Masters)

about three feet in the front. The school was located at a higher level so this wall did not block the view of Shama from observing Baba regularly.

Q. Did Baba ever recite *kalmas* from Quran as many Muslim devotees, Mullahs, and dervishes used to frequent Him?

A. Some Muslim devotees used to recite Quran inside Dwarkamayi Masjid before taking meals, particularly during lunch time. Baba also used to recite the sura (a chapter of Quran) appropriate for the occasion. This was not done when Hindu devotees were present during lunch.

Baba used to explain the fine nuances of Quran to the Muslim devotees and dervishes who used to frequent Him. Baba used to display certain characteristics of a Sufi saint. Abdul, who served Baba till His Maha Samadhi, has quoted a number of *kalmas* which, according to him, used to be recited by Shri Sai, which he claims to have recorded in his diary. I have studied this diary completely.

Q. What sort of books did Baba prescribe to His devotees to read?

A. Baba had the unique quality of knowing the mental traits of all His devotees. He used to prescribe different books to different devotees, according to their mental makeup and spiritual requirement. For example, He prescribed Bhagavat Gita to Bapu Saheb Jog and Bhagavat Purana to Kaka Mahajani. To other devotees, He used to suggest the intense study of religious books like Gyaneshwari, Ramayan, Ekanath Bhagavat, and many more. He prescribed reading of Adhyatma Ramayan and Ekanath Bhagavat to Kaka Saheb Dixit, Gita Rahasya to Lakshman, Guru Charitra to Kusa Bhav, Dasa Bodha and Yoga Vasishta to G. G. Narke,

Panchadasi to Upasani Maharaj, Upanishad Taittariya Bhaga to Mukund Lele Sastri, and Gyaneshwari to B. V. Dev.

When prescribing these books, He did not differentiate between His devotees on the basis of caste, creed, or clan. He did not make such prescriptions on any ground except the requirement of the devotee for his spiritual evolution.

> **Bhagavat Dharma**
>
> At the suggestion or recommendation of Sai Baba, Bapu Saheb Jog and Kaka Saheb Dixit read at Shirdi, daily, Bhagavat Gita with its Marathi commentary, Bhavartha Deepika or Gyaneshwari (a dialogue between Krishna and His friend-devotee, Arjuna), Nath Bhagavat (a dialogue between Krishna and His servant-devotee, Uddhava), and also Ekanath's other great work, Bhavartha Ramayan. When devotees came to Baba and asked Him certain questions, He sometimes answered them in part and asked them to go and listen to the readings of the above-mentioned works, which are the main treatises of Bhagavat Dharma. When the devotees went and listened, they got full and satisfactory replies to their questions. (Chapters 18 and 19, *Shri Sai Satcharita*)

Q. Baba is found to be wearing a white coloured Kafni (caftan) in photographs and paintings and a white headgear. Devotees used to give Him various other types of clothes. Did He wear any of these clothes?

A. When Shri Sai Baba first visited Shirdi as a young mendicant, He is said to have been wearing a loose and white cloth wrapped around the lower half of His body in an unusual manner, somewhat like wearing a dhoti. He also used to wear a headgear of green colour that was given to Him by His Guru as per His own admission. I am told that this piece of green cloth is in possession of Shri Shirdi Sai Sansthan, Shirdi.

During His early days at Shirdi, three local inhabitants named Kashiram Shimpi, Appa Jagle, and Mhalsapati became His close associates. Kashiram Shimpi presented Him a caftan, which He wore for a short period of time. After His defeat from Tamboli, a wrestler, in a wrestling bout at Shirdi, He started making exclusive use of the white Kafni and a white headgear. He wore this dress for the rest of His life and He entered Maha Samadhi in these clothes.

Radhakrishna Mai, a highly accomplished devotee, after her arrival at Shirdi, started collecting decorative items and refined clothes for Baba, which included silk caftans with golden and silver coloured embroidery. But Shirdi Sai never adorned any of these items. The spiritual Masters usually do not give any importance to purely material things like clothes and other items of comfort.

Q. What were the food habits of Baba? Did He have liking for any specific food?

A. A lot of information is available about Baba's food habits. Baba rarely displayed liking for any specific food. He ate whatever was offered to Him by the devotees. On His first arrival in Shirdi, Baija Maa used to feed Him with the usual food that people used to take in rural areas of Maharashtra, like *bhakri*, dal, etc. After He settled down in Dwarkamayi Masjid, He started begging food from a few houses regularly. Besides, devotees used to bring food cooked by them at home. The items included *bhakri, kachra, jhunka, puranpoli, seera*, cooked rice, dal, *ambli*, milk, curd, *channa*, and many more.

At times, Baba used to ask a devotee to prepare a certain food item. Baba Himself used to prepare food, both vegetarian and non-vegetarian (meat pulao), for His devotees, with minute care. There is no record to establish that He used to take non-vegetarian food and there is also no evidence to show that He dissuaded the devotees from taking non-vegetarian food. He used to partake of fruits like coconuts, guavas, bananas, mangoes, etc., offered by the devotees.

He was in the most detached state of mind and cannot be said to have attachment with any type of food. Many believe that even His asking for food from a certain devotee had a spiritual significance. Nevertheless, many Hindu devotees who came in contact with Him stopped taking non-vegetarian food and became vegetarians.

Baba's Handi

When He took it into His mind to distribute food to all, He made all preparations from beginning to end, Himself. He depended on nobody and troubled none in this matter. First, He went to the bazaar and bought all the things—corn, flour, spices, etc., for cash. He also did the grinding. In the open courtyard of the Masjid, He arranged a big hearth and after lighting a fire underneath, kept a *handi* over it, with a proper measure of water. There were two kinds of *handi*, one small and the other big. The former provided food for 50 persons, the later for 100. Sometimes He cooked "mitthe chaval" (sweet rice), and at other times "pulaava" (pulao) with meat. At times, in the boiling *varan* (soup), He put in small balls of thick or flat breads of wheat flour. He pounded the spices on a stone slab, and put the thin, pulverized spices into the cooking pot. He took all the pains to make the dishes very tasty. He prepared *ambli* by boiling jowar flour in water and mixing it with buttermilk. With the food He distributed this *ambli* to all alike. When the cooking was

> over, Baba brought the pots to the Masjid and had them duly consecrated by the moulvi. First, He sent a part of the food as prasad to Mhalsapati and Tatya Patil and then He served the remaining contents with His own hands to all the poor and helpless people who could eat to their hearts' content.
>
> Somebody may raise a doubt here and ask, "Did Baba distribute vegetable and animal food as prasad alike to all His devotees?" The answer is plain and simple. Those who were accustomed to (take) animal food, were given food from the *handi* as prasad and those who were not so accustomed, were not allowed to touch it. (Chapter 38, *Shri Sai Satcharita*)

Q. Why is the day of Shri Ram Jayanti celebrated as the birthday of Sai Baba? Was Baba born on a Ram Navami day?

A. Shirdi Sai Baba has not divulged the secrets of His date of birth, place of birth, and parentage. Therefore, it cannot be conclusively asserted that He was born on the day of Ram Navami. Even Dasganu Maharaj, who had visited many places like Pathri and Selu villages to unearth the mystery shrouding Baba's birth and parentage, could not get any reliable information. One researcher has floated an idea that He was born on September 28, 1838. Going back in Hindu calendar, we find that even this day does not coincide with the day of Ram Navami.

I will try to reply to this query, taking into consideration the significance of Ram Navami at Shirdi during the time of Baba and draw my conclusions. Shri Rama, considered to be an incarnation in Hinduism, is widely worshiped in Maharashtra. We hear about the concepts of Rama Dasi, Guru Ram Das, the Spiritual Guru of King Shivaji, etc. In Shirdi, due to the encouragement shown by Baba, Ram Navami day used to be celebrated with a lot of fanfare and joy. Besides the entire population of Shirdi, people from the neighbouring villages also used to participate in large numbers. Even the Muslim community used to play an active and friendly role in the festival. On this day, besides worshiping Lord Rama, devotees used to worship Baba as well. Some devotees are said to have experienced Baba in the form of Shri Rama when He used to be at Dwarkamayi Masjid. Baba had given vision to many devotees in many forms, for example, Shri Vishnu, Shri Dattatreya, and Shri Rama. Baba used to love and protect all His devotees as Shri Rama used to love and protect His devotees. Given this background, it was natural for the devotees to celebrate the day of Ram Navami as Baba's birth day. Shri Sai Satcharita narrates in detail regarding the significance and celebration of Ram Navami.

Urs Transformed into Ram Navami

In 1912, a change took place. That year a devotee, Krishnarao Jageshwar Bhisma (the author of the pamphlet *Sai Sagunopasana*), came to the fair with Dada Saheb Khaparde of Amravati and was staying on the previous day at the Dixit Wada. While he was lying in the verandah, and while Lakshmanrao, alias Kaka Mahajani, was going down with puja material to the Masjid, a new thought arose in his mind and he accosted the latter thus—There is some providential arrangement in the fact that the Urs or fair is celebrated in Shirdi on the Ram Navami day; this day is very dear to all the Hindus; then why not begin the Ram Navami Festival, the celebration of the birth of Shri Rama, here on this day? Kaka Mahajani liked the idea, and it was arranged to get

Baba's permission in this matter. So they immediately went to the Masjid to get Baba's permission. Baba, who knew all things and what was passing there, asked Mahajani, as to what was going on in the Wada. Being rather perturbed, Mahajani could not catch the purpose of the question and remained silent. Then Baba asked Bhisma what he had to say. He explained the idea of celebrating Ram Navami festival and asked for Baba's permission and Baba gladly gave it. All rejoiced and made preparations for the jayanti festival.

Since 1912, this festival began to grow gradually, year by year. From the 8th to 12th of *Chaitra*, Shirdi looked like a beehive of men. Shops began to increase. Celebrated wrestlers took part in wrestling bouts. Feeding of the poor was done on a grander scale. Hard work and sincere efforts of Radhakrishna Mai turned Shirdi into a *Sansthan* (State). Paraphernalia increased. A beautiful horse, a palanquin, chariot, and many silver articles, pots, buckets, pictures, mirrors, etc., were presented. Elephants were also sent for the procession. Though all this paraphernalia increased enormously, Sai Baba ignored all these things and maintained His simplicity as before.

It is to be noted that both the Hindus and Mahomedans have been working in unison in both the processions, and during the entire festival there has been no hitch or quarrel between them at all so far. First, about 5,000–7,000 people used to collect, but that figure went up to 75,000 in some years; still there was no outbreak of any epidemic or any riots worth the name during the past so many years. (Chapter 6, *Shri Sai Satcharita*)

Q. What was the role of Radhakrishna Mai in the affairs of Baba?

A. Radhakrishna Mai came to Baba as a young, 26 year old widow in the year 1907 and left her body at Shirdi in 1916. She was a lady with many accomplishments in the fields of religion, music, cooking, service to the poor, domestic management, and even yogic practices. She used to stay in the house located in front of Chavadi, where the family of Abdul, an ardent devotee of Baba, is presently settled. Radhakrishna Mai used to worship Baba as Lord Krishna in the form of a devotional cult of Krishna worship which she had imbibed from her family.

She rarely approached Baba face to face. Every day, she would cook some food and send it to Baba. Baba would send her back one chapati. She would only eat what Baba sent to her each day and continue with her spiritual practices. It was Radhakrishna Mai who was instrumental in organizing decorated and silk clothes, palanquin, and other items of opulence through other devotees for Baba. Baba never used these items. He never sat in the palanquin.

Baba used to send some of the devotees to Radhakrishna Mai for taking shelter at her place during their visit to Shirdi. She was being treated as a Guru and a mother by Justice Rege and some others. Her house was full of costly and decorative items collected by her for the use of Baba. After her death, these items were handed over to Rao Bahadur Sathe as a trustee of the property. Rao Bahadur Sathe, by then, had created an organization named Dakshina Bhiksha Sansthan. These items were later handed over to the Shirdi Sai Sansthan after it was formed in 1921.

One Radhakrishna Ayi, a young widow of the family name of Sahasrabuddhe, came and established herself as a devotee of Baba, and being highly accomplished, was intent upon using all her gifts and cleverness for developing Sai Baba's worship. She drew a large number of people to herself and made them more enthusiastic in the cause of Sai worship. She made them carry out her plan of fitting out Baba and His Chavadi in exactly the same way as these would be fitted out if Baba was a real Maharaja and a real God's image.... Radhakrishna Mai introduced silver whisks, silver maces, silver umbrellas, silver candelabras, moons, and artificial gardens to deck the Chavadi where Baba was worshipped on alternate nights. A car, a palanquin with silver appurtenances, a horse, and other regal paraphernalia were furnished on her insistence and the insistence of other devotees to make Baba worship run exactly like Vithal worship.

Baba had no possessions and all these regal paraphernalia mentioned above were kept with Mai and on her death, were held by an association, and finally vested in the Sai Sansthan, formed by the order of the Ahmednagar District Court in the year 1922. (Chapter 6, Part I, *Life of Sai Baba* by Narasimha Swami, p. 32)

Radhakrishna Mai served in all possible ways. Twice in the day she swept and cleared the path on which Maharaj walked. Consequently, she herself removed all the dirt there. Before her, this work had been started by Balaji Patil Nevaskar.

Not only did Radhakrishna Mai render all kinds of services to Maharaj, but got several of Maharaj's devotees to do all kinds of services. She did various kinds of chores; and got all involved in them; and the devotees did the work with love and eagerness. Men of all status, and

> also women, were included in that. To carry away earth and stones, sweeping roads, making mud and carrying it, digging trenches and filling them, splitting wood, dusting lamps and chandeliers, washing and painting the Masjid, making flowers from paper, holding whisks, peacock feather fans, ornamental umbrellas, flags, stitching flags—all these were done by people of higher status and even ladies coming from noble families who were all pleased to have got the opportunity to render service. (*Sai Leela*, 1923, Ank 1)

Q. When did the Palki Yatra start in Shirdi? What is its significance?

A. A *palki* or palanquin is a conveyance which consists of an enclosed litter, borne on the shoulder of men by means of poles. In India, it is being used since the ancient times to carry the rich, royal, and powerful people and also Gurus and saints. Statues or paintings of the deities of the Hindu pantheon also used to be carried in palkis on days of religious significance.

Following this ancient Hindu tradition, some devotees of Shri Sai Baba introduced this tradition at Shirdi, on December 9, 1910. Before this day, Baba used to sleep only in the Dwarkamayi Masjid, but on this day he proceeded to Chavadi and slept there. The next morning, He returned to Dwarkamayi in a procession.

From this day onwards, Baba started sleeping in Dwarkamayi and Chavadi on alternate days. Even though the distance between these two places was a few steps, the devotees wished to carry Baba, sitting in a palki, on their shoulders. This was a way of expression of their love. However, Baba never sat in the palki when going from Dwarkamayi to Chavadi. His picture used to be carried in the palki; He used to walk in the procession, with jubilant devotees, with the fanfare of

Shirdi Sai Baba and Sadgurus (Perfect Masters)

assorted musical instruments, singing of bhajans, and chanting the name of Shri Sai. In due course of time, this procession became a part and parcel of the life of the inhabitants of Shirdi and of the visiting devotees of Baba. Detailed description about this procession can be found in Shri Sai Satcharita.

The tradition of palki procession continues at Shirdi, with the difference that it is taken out only on Thursdays. Taking out a palki with Baba's picture or photograph in a procession, particularly on Thursdays, has become a tradition in many Sai temples.

Sai Baba used to encourage group worship, group feeding, and participation of various people in festivals and religious functions. Palki Yatra is one such event which developed friendship and goodwill among people belonging to different religions, castes, and creeds.

Q. These days gold is being donated by devotees at Shirdi. Baba never wanted any of these items saying, "Bhau, why all this? I have nothing except a tin pot and a chillum, and I am a poor fakir. Don't get these attachments to me." Then, why donate gold?

A. When Baba was in Shirdi, all sorts of people, both rich and poor, used to visit Him. They offered Him whatever they could like coconuts, sweets, garlands, flowers, silver coins, gold jewellery, and many other costly items. Baba was in a *nirguna* state, which means, He was beyond the attraction of these materials. He used to accept whatever the devotees gave, but distributed these items to others. The rich people used to give gold and silver and the poor used to give coconuts or sweets and coins. He distributed his love equally to all. Therefore, it does not matter what the devotees offer to Baba. Baba never encouraged the gift of costly items, but when given to Him, distributed them to the devotees who benefited from them. He never treated a devotee on the basis of what he offered. The rich and poor, all were given equal treatment by Baba, notwithstanding whether they offered anything or not. Baba's view was that He accepted anything from anyone as per directions of Allah and not otherwise. The following paragraph reveals Baba's attitude towards the material aspect of life:

> Purandhare and his friends had, with great enthusiasm and trouble, secured for Baba's picture a silver palanquin with silver ornaments tacked on to the top of the same, but, when these were brought by the loving and enthusiastic devotees, Baba, who hated all pomp and pageantry and rated them at their proper worth, refused to allow the palanquin to be brought into His mosque, as Baba Himself would not sit in a palki. He said, "Let it remain outside" and so the whole night, the palki remained outside without any watchman. During the night, some thieves came and made away some of the silver horses. In the morning, the much distraught devotees ran to Baba and complained about the theft. Baba simply said, "Why did the thieves not take away the whole palanquin?" Baba had so much contempt for wealth. But the devotees would not give up their own notions as to the need for wealth and pomp to set off Sai Baba as a real Maharaja, a Prince, with all sorts of appurtenance like silver palanquin. (Chapter 1, Part III, *Life of Sai Baba* by Narasimha Swami, p. 488)
>
> Once Kaka Saheb Dixit got a trunk full of rupees (maybe ₹ 1,000), which he earned in a Native State and he placed it before Baba saying, "Baba, all this is yours." Baba at once distributed the entire amount to the crowd around, while Dixit watched quietly, without reaction, which any ordinary mortal would not have taken with

such equanimity. (Chapter 4, Part II, *Life of Sai Baba* by Narasimha Swami p. 337)

Q. Shirdi Sai Baba often used to demand dakshina from some of the devotees, but not from all. Did He follow a pattern when demanding dakshina or did He do it on a random basis?

A. Most of the information available on Shri Shirdi Sai Baba in different books, magazines, and internet websites highlights about the Master's demand of money as dakshina from his devotees and others who used to visit Him. This used to happen in many ways: a) Baba used to demand dakshina directly from the devotee who used to visit Him, b) He demanded dakshina from one devotee, by sending a message through another devotee, c) He accepted dakshina when offered by a devotee from his side without asking, d) He refused to accept dakshina, when offered by a devotee, e) In case of *a* and *c* above, He demanded repeated dakshina from some devotees, f) He accepted dakshina on the basis of indication given to the devotee in a dream, g) He read the thoughts of the devotee and demanded dakshina accordingly, h) He demanded dakshina from devotees when they completed certain pious acts like reading of a *Pothi*, etc.

It has been found that the act of giving or taking of dakshina was not a simple act. At times, it was a mystical act by Baba, to give some sort of a benefit to His devotee. Often, He used to say that He demanded and took dakshina only from those persons from whom Allah desired Him to take.

Many authors have tried to correlate the number of coins demanded by Baba from a devotee with numerical correlations in the spiritual world, for example, Baba taking or even giving nine coins to devotee means he demanded Navadha Bhakti.

Kashiram Shimpi was the first person who gave dakshina to Baba. Every morning, he would bring 1 or 2 paisa and lay it at Baba's feet. At that time, Baba did not accept any money offerings from the devotees. Baba, however, accepted the money offered by Kashiram Shimpi, as it was offered with love and devotion.

At a later stage, Kashiram started placing his entire income before Baba. He used to affectionately insist that Baba should give back whatever money He wished. Baba used to keep only a paisa or two and return the rest. Kashiram was very much hurt when Baba either did not take any money or took very little.

A person may feel proud that he has the ability to give. Such a feeling is harmful for the spiritual advancement. Hence, Baba either refused to keep any money or took a very meagre amount. Gradually, the seed of pride took hold of Kashiram Shimpi and he felt that he was the provider of Baba's needs. At that moment, his financial condition started declining and Baba's demands for dakshina started increasing. Finally, he had to tell Baba that he did not have the money. A lesson had to be taught, so Baba asked him to borrow the money. After a while, the creditors refused to give him money and then he realized that he was not the provider of Baba's needs. Due to this insistence, Kashiram lost his feeling of false pride and then his monetary situation started improving. (*Sai Leela*, 1923, Ank 1)

Baba asked S. B. Dhumal to give ₹ 50 as dakshina. Dhumal said I have not got the money. Then Baba told him to ask Saheb (H.V.S. – Hari Vinayak Sathe). Dhumal went and asked H.V.S. for ₹ 50; H.V.S. gladly gave it. This was an indication to H.V.S. that his claim, then pending before Government, for an extra sum of ₹ 50 as part of

Shirdi Sai Baba and Sadgurus (Perfect Masters) 121

> his pension was to be allowed. Later, the order allowing it came. And the date of the order was the date of Baba's demand of ₹ 50. (*Sri Sai Baba's Charters and Sayings* by Narasimha Swami, p. 92)
>
> Gajanan Narvekar, who was getting high fever, sent his son to Shirdi with ₹ 500 as dakshina. As soon as this dakshina was paid to Sai Baba, He started shivering and got fever. Sai Baba said, "I have to carry the burden of him whose dakshina I accept." (*Sai Sharan Anand Shri Sai Baba*, Translated by V. B. Kher, p. 273)

Q. **With so many devotees visiting Him every day, Baba must have accumulated a lot of money. How did He spend it?**

A. When asked on the issue of dakshina, Baba's explanation was succinct and clear. His observations, made at different points of time to different devotees, can be summed up in the following five points: 1) He used to take anything, including monetary donation or other types of dakshina from anyone whom Allah directed Him to take, but not from others. 2) He did not take anything for free. Whatever He took, He returned ten times over, in various ways, known or unknown to the devotees. This means, He returns it manifold. 3) His give-and-take relationship with some devotees is a carry forward of the relationship of the past lives. 4) Being a fakir, without the encumbrances of a family, He had no reason to hoard anything—money or material. He used the opportunity of giving or taking of dakshina to annihilate the ego of His devotees, to give immediate help, and also to grow their virtue. 5) Fakiri, which believes in distribution of wealth to the less fortunate souls, is the real kingship on earth and not possessions. He used to distribute the entire amount that He used to receive as dakshina by the end of the day.

He used to distribute the dakshina money to some like Bade Baba and Tatya on a daily basis and to others occasionally. Besides giving donation to His devotees out of the dakshina money, some amount was being spent for other purposes like purchase of food items and Chillum Tamakhu (tobacco) for Baba and others, one time help given to visitors for their stay at Shirdi, transport cost to some poor devotees who had no money to go back home, reward to performing artists and rural acrobats, and for many other purposes which helped the devotees immensely. Baba never kept any money with Him. However, some of the recipients like Bade Baba and Tatya received so much from Baba that they had to pay income tax on their earning.

When He took His Maha Samadhi on October 15, 1918, He had only seven coins in His pocket, after He had given away nine silver coins to Lakshmi Bai Shinde moments before His Maha Samadhi.

With a very large daily income, he left only ₹ 16 at the moment of His passing away from His body. (Chapter 4, Part III, *Life of Sai Baba* by B. V. Narasimha Swami, p. 526)

When Baba left the body, He had only ₹ 16 in his hand and no other property. (Chapter 5, Part I, *Life of Sai Baba* by B. V. Narasimha Swami, p. 36)

Kaka Mahajani's Master

Then Baba asked Kaka for ₹ 15 as dakshina and received it. To Kaka, He said, "If I take one rupee as dakshina from anybody I have to return it tenfold to him. I never take anything gratis. I never ask anyone indiscriminately. I only ask and take from him whom the Fakir (My Guru) points out. If anyone is indebted formerly to the Fakir, money is received from him. The donor gives, that is, sows his seeds, only to reap a rich harvest in future. Wealth should be the means to work out Dharma. The giving of dakshina advances *vairagya* (non-attachment) and thereby bhakti and gyan. Give one and receive tenfold." (Chapter 35, *Shri Sai Satcharita*)

Dakshina Mimansa

To quote an instance, Ganpatrao Bodas, the famous actor, says in his Marathi autobiography that on Baba's pressing him often and often for dakshina, he emptied his money-bag before Him. The result of this was, as Bodas says, that in later life he never lacked money, as it came to him abundantly. (Chapter 14, *Shri Sai Satcharita*)

Behaviour of Sai Baba

He got almost all the temples in Shirdi repaired. Through Tatya Patil, the temples of Shani, Ganapati, Shankar-Parvati, Village Deity, and Maruti were put in order. His charity was also remarkable. The money He used to collect as dakshina was freely distributed, ₹ 20 to some, ₹ 15 or 50 to others, every day. (Chapter 7, *Shri Sai Satcharita*)

Monetary Donation by Baba

A lot of money in the form of dakshina was collected daily by Sai Baba and out of this amount, He gave daily one rupee to a three year old girl, Amani, the daughter of Bhakta Kondaji, ₹ 2 to 5 to some, ₹ 6 to Jamali, the mother of Amani, and ₹ 10 to 20 and even ₹ 50 to other Bhaktas as He pleased. (Chapter 29, *Shri Sai Satcharita*)

Q. Shirdi Sai Baba, at times, used to utter strong and even abusive language when communicating with His devotees. At one moment, He used to shower love and the next moment, abuse. Is it natural for a Sadguru to behave in this manner?

A. Various writings on Baba in books, journals, and personal memoirs of devotees indicate that, at times, He would resort to the use of intemperate language. However, it is found that He was not selective in the use of such language. It is also reported that His moods used to change suddenly, which generally may be termed as "mood swings". When he would be in such a mood, devotees would get scared and leave His proximity. From a general point of view, such reactions on the part of the devotees appear to be logical. The main point that needs to be understood is the reason for the demonstration of such behaviour of a Sadguru, who is full of compassion and ever helpful to His devotees. The spiritual Masters, as per Sufi theory, sometimes remain in a *jamali* state (peaceful state) and, at times, exhibit the *jalali* state (agitated state) of mind. When in this state of mind, they demonstrate strange behaviour. They even become violent and abusive.

Baba used to show the state of *jamali* and *jalali* both. In a moment, He would be enraged and at the next moment, he would become extremely peaceful.

The Sadgurus usually exhibit one of the four states of behaviour, that is, of a child, of a gyani (with silence), of a mad man, or a ghoul (*preta*). At times, their intense compassion to protect their devotees creates such powerful upsurge of emotions that their body fails to hold these emotions. In such a stage, their language and the features of their body become uncontrollable and even violent.

To understand this critical thought, let us take the example of how Baba behaved with Shama when he was bitten by a snake.

Shama Cured of a Snake-Bite

Once Shama was bitten by a poisonous snake. Shama ran to the Masjid. When Baba saw him, He began to scold and abuse. He got enraged and said, "Oh, vile *Bhaturdya* (priest), do not climb up. Beware if you do so." And then He roared, "Go, Get away, Come down." Seeing Baba thus red with wrath, Shama was greatly puzzled and disappointed. He thought that the Masjid was his home and Sai Baba his sole refuge, but if he was driven away like this, where should he go? He lost all hope of life and kept silent. After some time, Baba became normal and calm when Shama went up and sat near Him. Then Baba said to him, "Don't be afraid, don't care a jot, the Merciful Fakir will save you, go and sit quietly at home, don't go out, believe in Me and remain fearless and have no anxiety."

The only thing to be remembered in this connection is this — the words of Baba (or the five syllabled mantra, that is, "Go, Get away, Come down") were not addressed to Shama — as it apparently looked — but they were a direct order to the snake and its poison not to go up and circulate through Shama's body. (Chapter 23, *Shri Sai Satcharita*)

11

Spiritual Education

Q. In the existing system of formal education, a student comes to know about the level of his educational proficiency through the help of markers like the scores or grades awarded by teachers on different subjects. What are the markers in the field of spiritual knowledge that can help a pupil to understand the stage of his spiritual evolution?

A. Let us examine the case of a prominent disciple of Shirdi Sai Baba by the name of Shri Kaka Saheb Dixit. He visited Baba for the first time on November 2, 1909. A rich and well placed solicitor of Mumbai, who was successful in all material aspects of life, he came to Baba to cure his lame leg, caused by a train accident when he was in London. But after meeting Baba, he requested Him to cure the lameness of his mind instead (forgetting to ask for curing the lameness of his body) for the rest of the life. He was so attracted by Baba that he virtually lived at Shirdi with Him for the rest of his life. He followed every instruction of Baba, both in letter and in spirit.

Readers of Shri Sai Satcharita will do well to remember the incident depicted in the book in which Baba tried to test the faith of His devotees. Once, Baba asked some of His close devotees like Shama, Bade Baba, and others to kill a goat. None of them tried to carry out the orders of Baba, citing different pretexts, except Kaka Saheb Dixit. Nobody could have ever imagined that Kaka Saheb would think of killing a goat as he was a chaste Brahmin and a vegetarian in food habits. Following the Guru's orders, he was about to strike the goat with a long knife, when Baba stopped him from doing so. When asked about this incident, Kaka said that he believed only in following the orders of the Guru without any consideration of its consequences.

He came out successful in the test set for him by his Guru, whereas other prominent devotees failed. What were the markers in this test? The markers were shraddha, which means complete faith in Baba, and saburi, which stands for patience in carrying out the difficult orders of the Guru. Kaka Saheb Dixit passed the test with flying colours, whereas others failed.

The Spiritual Masters periodically takes the test of the devotees through such direct methods. They don't ask the students to write answers on an answer sheet. Unlike the existing system of formal education, where both written and practical tests are taken by the students, in the system of spiritual education, there is always a direct way of testing the knowledge of the disciple.

Q. **Is there any difference between the existing system of education and the system of spiritual education imparted by the saints and Sadgurus?**

A. In the existing system of education followed in schools, colleges, and universities, the level of achievement of a student is judged through a system of awarding marks in the opted subjects. The prevalent system of education, besides the student, requires the involvement of a number of teachers, question-setters, and examiners. On the other hand, the Sadguru or the Spiritual Master plays all the three roles of the teacher, question-setter, and examiner in the spiritual education of the devotees. The formal system of education is run by professional teachers who take payment for imparting education, out of the fees paid by the students. The relationship of such teachers with the students is limited to a few scheduled classes during the educational calendar. The formal system of education imparts only an indirect form of education with a limited purpose. It is meant to develop the skill, knowledge, and attitude of the student. It is an exercise to be successful in the materialistic world. Generally, it creates a formal relationship between the student and the teacher, with little emotional relationship.

On the other hand, the relationship between a Sadguru and His disciple is a highly emotional one and spreads over the whole life or a few lives. Spiritual education gives direct experience and knowledge pertaining to the seen and unseen universe, nature, and God. The purpose of the spiritual education is not for earning livelihood, as is the case with the formal education. It is for the spiritual evolution of the disciple. The student, on the completion of his spiritual education, takes the responsibility of imparting similar education to his deserving pupils when he takes over the role of a Guru.

The disciples of the Sadgurus go out into the world to serve the poor, destitute, miserable, confused, and the oppressed people. They expect no material returns for the services they render.

12

Experiences

Q. **Devotees believe that their visit to Shirdi takes place when Baba so desires. Some people frequent Shirdi with ease and get quick darshan, but others find it difficult to do so. Why is there such a difference?**

A. This is one of the problems which some devotees face when they visit temples, ashrams, or durbars. They have to wait for long hours in the queue, sometimes under the most inconvenient circumstances. If we go through the history of religious movements in the world, including those in India, this aspect will shine prominently. Such negative emotions arise in the minds of some of the devotees when they feel that they are treated differently from other devotees in the religious places, where everyone should be treated equally. However, the best devotees, who have full faith in Baba, do not entertain such feelings in their mind. Sadgurus or the Spiritual Masters know the inner thoughts and feelings of all. They know about those devotees who need their immediate attention and those who don't. They also take into consideration, the stock of *punya* (virtues) and *paapa* (vices) carried forward from the *prarabdha* (past life) of each of the disciples and devotees.

Shirdi Sai Baba's approach to some of the devotees, at times, used to be quite contrary to the general expectation. For example, when a Haji by the name of Sidik Falke, on return from Haj, came to Shirdi and insisted on meeting Baba in the Dwarkamayi Masjid, he was not allowed to do so for about nine months. Many devotees requested Baba, many numbers of times, to meet him, but Baba did not do so and went on rebuking him. However, when the appropriate time arrived, He Himself went and met the Haji with gifts. Thereafter, the Haji was allowed to visit Baba regularly.

It is difficult to comprehend such inscrutable behaviour on the part of Baba. Perhaps, Baba wanted to lower his pride of being a Haji and a learned person. Nevertheless, the Haji, in his spiritual pursuits during his stay at Shirdi, immensely benefited from Baba.

There are many such examples which have been codified in Shri Sai Satcharita.

A real devotee will always wait for his turn to visit the Master, instead of feeling vexed, jealous, or frustrated if he does not get an easy appointment with Him. A person who has staunch faith (shraddha) and patience (saburi), will surely wait for the Guru to call him.

Q. **At times, the family members of some of the devotees, who are not the devotees of Baba, object to his visit to Sai temples and his participation in functions relating to Baba. How should we handle such a situation?**

A. When Baba was at Shirdi, a few devotees used to face the same problem which some face today. Baba would often query about the family members of a devotee, but He would never force the devotee to prevail upon his relatives to bring them to Him.

The history of the Sai movement shows that some of the genuine followers of Baba had to face many difficulties, including those created by the family members. It is said that such situations are created by the Guru or the divine powers in order to strengthen the faith and patience of the devotees by exposing them to such difficulties.

Devotion towards the Guru is entirely a personal matter. If any family member shows an adverse reaction to such a personal matter, it is better not to try to convince him through arguments, because faith cannot be built through the application of dry logic and arguments. Devotion is an inner feeling of the heart. However, often, in Baba's time as well as now, the same non-believers start believing in Baba in due course of time.

Therefore, a true devotee should bear such social disapprobation with equanimity and patience and pray to Baba to evoke the right thoughts in the minds of such ignorant people. After all, they are family members and have to be handled with love and caution. You may like to persuade them to visit Baba's Samadhi Mandir at Shirdi and experience the divinity of Baba and His divine influence on lakhs and lakhs of devotees.

But forceful imposition of one's faith on them is likely to generate an adverse reaction. When replying to their queries and clarifying their doubts, we have to be polite and soft in approach, without showing any negative reactions. The Sadguru knows how and when to pull His disciple towards Him.

Kaka Mahajani's Friend

A friend of Kaka Mahajani was a worshipper of God without form and was averse to idolatry. Out of curiosity, he agreed to go to Shirdi with Kaka Mahajani on two conditions—he would neither bow to Baba, nor pay Him any dakshina. Kaka agreed to these conditions and both of them left Mumbai on a Saturday night and reached Shirdi the next morning. As soon as they put their feet on the steps of the Masjid, Baba, looking at the friend from a little distance, addressed him in sweet words as follows: "Oh, welcome sir." The tone of these words was very peculiar. It exactly resembled the tone of the friend's father. This reminded him of his departed father and sent a thrill of joy through his body. What an enchanting power the tone had! Being surprised, the friend said, "This is no doubt the voice of my father." Then he at once got up and, forgetting his resolution, placed his head upon Baba's feet. (Chapter 35, *Shri Sai Satcharita*)

A Doctor

Once a Mamlatdar came to Shirdi with a doctor friend. The doctor said that his deity was Rama and that he would not bow before a Mahomedan, and so he was unwilling to go to Shirdi. The Mamlatdar replied that nobody would press him to make a bow, nor even ask him to do so. So he could come and give the pleasure of his company. Accordingly, they came to Shirdi and went to the Masjid for Baba's darshan. All were wonderstruck to see the doctor going ahead and saluting Baba. They asked him how he forgot his resolve and bowed before a Mussalman. The doctor replied that he saw his beloved deity, Rama, on the seat and he, therefore, prostrated himself before Him. Then, as he was saying this, he saw Sai Baba there, instead. Being amazed, he said, "Is this a dream? How could He be a Mahomedan? He is a great Yogasampanna (full of yoga) Avatar." (Chapter 12, *Shri Sai Satcharita*)

Q. **All the devotees of Baba do not experience His presence in the same manner. What is the reason behind this?**

A. The impact of Baba on the life of a devotee and the devotee's experiences with relation to Him depend on the priority and importance that he gives to Baba in his life. We need to place Baba at the centre of His existence and heart in order to be close to Him and experience His divinity in different ways. The depth of devotion of the devotee towards Baba will affect the experience of the devotee accordingly. A portion of Baba's Aarti says the same thing, "*Jaya mani jaisa bhava, taya taisa anubhaba.*" It is also believed that some devotees who had a relation with Baba in their past lives will experience Him better than others.

Dictum of Goulibuva

An old devotee by name Goulibuva, aged about 95 years, was a Varkari of Pandhari. He stayed eight months at Pandharpur and four months — *Ashadha* to *Kartik* (July-November) — on the banks of the Ganges. He had an ass with him for carrying his luggage, and a disciple as his companion. Every year, he made his *vari* or trip to Pandharpur and came to Shirdi to see Sai Baba, Whom he loved the most. He used to stare at Baba and say, "This is Pandharinath Vithal incarnate, the Merciful Lord of the poor and helpless." This Goulibuva was an old devotee of Vithoba and had made many a trip to Pandhari; and he testified that Sai Baba was the real Pandharinath. (Chapter 4, *Shri Sai Satcharita*)

Wonderful Vision

Things were going on like this, when the husband got a wonderful vision in his dreams one night. He was in a big city, the police there had arrested him, tied his hands with a rope, and put him up in a cage (lock-up). As the police were tightening the rope, he saw Sai Baba standing quietly outside, near the cage. On seeing Baba so near, he said in a plaintive tone, "Hearing Your fame I came to Your feet. Why should this calamity befall me when You are standing here in person?" Baba replied, "You must suffer the consequences of your actions." He said, "I have not done anything in this life which would bring such a misfortune on me." Baba replied, "If not in this life, you must have committed some sin in your past life." He said, "I do not know anything of my past life, but assuming that I did commit some sin then, why should it not be burnt and destroyed in Your presence, as dry grass before fire?" Baba replied, "Have you got such faith?" He said, "Yes." Baba then asked him to close his eyes. No sooner had he shut them than he heard a thumping sound of something falling down, and on opening his eyes, he saw that he was free and the policeman had fallen down bleeding. Being much frightened, he began to look at Baba, who said, "Now you are well caught. Officers will now come and arrest you." Then he begged, "There is no other saviour except You, save me anyhow." Baba asked him to close his eyes again. He did so and when he opened them, he saw that he was free, out of the cage, and that Baba was by his side. He then fell at Baba's feet. Baba asked him, "Is there any difference between this namaskar and your previous ones? Think well and reply." He said, "There is a lot of difference; my former namaskars were offered with the object of getting money from You, but the present namaskar is one offered to You as God. (Chapter 4, *Shri Sai Satcharita*)

Sadguru is like a Mirror
(91 and 92)

The image of the devotee is reflected in the Guru when the devotee comes near Him. The Sadguru reacts according to the thought processes of the devotee. At times, He seems to be in a rage, smashing some material

> objects. He even showers abuses or throws stones at the devotees.
>
> **(93 and 94)**
>
> His reactions are usually peaceful towards a pure devotee, but in a crooked person, it awakens fear. He is full of parental affection for the children. He is satirical when treating an egocentric person. However, in all His activities, the Guru (solely) is driven by kindness even when He sometimes acts in a manner which generates great surprise.
>
> (Vol. II, *Shri Guru Bhagavat*, English translation by Chandra Bhanu Satpathy)

Q. How can we overcome obstructions and receive subtle indications from Baba?

A. Sometimes, the word "subtle" in the spiritual parlance is used as a synonym for "mystique" and "spiritual". The evil mental proclivities (*kusanskars*), ego, and *prarabdha* debts are so strongly entrenched in the human psyche that it takes many lives for the devotees to become free of them. When the mind is so occupied with gross realities, how can it receive the subtle signals and advice from the Guru?

The disciples of the Guru have to make themselves worthy of being able to properly capture and interpret His instructions, expressed in a subtle language. Some devotees have the tendency to derive their own conclusions from the teachings of the Guru. They colour the words of the Master according to their own wishes. First, we have to always strive to dilute the base or gross mental and physical tendencies, conceptions, and complexes by practicing the enforcement of good thoughts, conduct, and behaviour. We have to annihilate one's ego wilfully. We have to reduce the burden of our karmic debts by bearing its consequences with forbearance. Only when the mind gets cleansed can the subtle indications of the Sadguru be clearly understood. Through the proper understanding of these indications, and by conducting oneself accordingly, we can escape difficulties and sorrows and also evolve spiritually.

Q. If "Dharma" is truth, then I find it to be difficult to be truthful and practise Dharma in life. What should I do?

A. In the complex society of today, it is not easy for an ordinary human being to be truthful in the purest sense of the term. To be truthful doesn't necessarily mean to divulge uncalled for information or to blurt out secrets to all and sundry, because it may cause harm to the speaker.

What is the basic idea of being truthful? Truthfulness, if practised by all the individuals living in a society, will reduce individual and social conflicts and create a better social order for the benefit, not only of the individuals, but the society as a whole. However, a statement of truth made only for the purpose of proving that we are truthful is likely to cause harm to the speaker and others as well. What is the value of uttering such a truth? If we go through the epic Mahabharata, we will find that even an incarnation like Lord Krishna had tread the path of Dharma or truthfulness with extreme caution. The Pandavas, who tried to follow Dharma, had to go through unimaginable difficulties.

We should shun uttering lies which harm others and our own self in the long run. Some people are often found to speak lies as a habit (known as compulsive liars) or to take resort to falsehood in order to satisfy their ego. For example, somebody asks someone about the value of the ornament he is wearing. It is found that instead of telling the actual value, some people, just to show off, mention a greater value. Telling lies on small issues like this on a daily basis becomes a second habit for such individuals in the due course of time. Very few people are aware about the number of such small and big lies they speak, unconsciously, in their routine communications with others. Most of such false utterances are of no benefit to anyone. Hence, we must avoid speaking such lies, as well as focusing on telling the truth. They are two sides of the same coin.

Q. Should we not tell the truth even if it hurts the listener?

A. Usually, very few people want to listen about high ideals and truths, particularly when such truths are expressed in a language and a style which is unpalatable. Speaking the truth does not necessary require the use of harsh or unsavoury language. However, before advising others to follow this dictum, we must find out whether we apply such a moral conduct in our own life. For instance, how can a person, who consumes alcohol, convince his children that taking alcohol is harmful to health? How will children adopt good habits unless their parents lead them by example?

Truth is a reality and not an imaginary creation of mind. However, even when telling a truth, we have to be extremely cautious about the use of the appropriate words, language, and gestures. There is a beautiful Sanskrit *shloka* which says, "*Satyam bruyat, priyam bruyat, ma bruyat satyamapriyam.*" This means, "Speak the truth and speak what is pleasant to listen, but don't speak truth in a manner that is unpleasant."

When we hurt the feelings of a person, even if telling the truth, we create for ourselves a negative value known as "*sukshma paapa*". The act of communication lies in telling the truth, but in a manner that it does not hurt the feelings of the listener.

13

Questions from International Devotees

Q. Recently, I got a small idol of Shri Shirdi Sai. My husband and I go to work and we have children. Please inform us the way to worship the statue of Sai Baba at home under these circumstances.

A. If both the husband and wife are working in the US, and have children to look after, it is neither possible nor feasible to worship Baba in the same manner in which puja is performed by the devotees in India. I know that both of you, and also the children, will have to get up early in the morning and leave home, even before sunrise, particularly during the winter season. The working hours in US often begin at 8:00 a.m. and end at 5:00 p.m.

In your situation, one of the partners will have to take the responsibility to clean Baba's statue; anoint it with sandal or vermillion; place a few flowers; offer a fruit, dry fruit, or even candy; recite Sai Mantra or aarti; and take a little Udi, if available, as prasad. The entire process does not take more than ten minutes — a small period of time which you can easily afford.

After returning home in the evening, one of the partners can light a smoke-free candle before Baba, offer dry prasad or cooked food, and perform aarti. If it is not possible to recite the entire aarti, a portion of it can be recited. This is known as *Chhoti Aarti* by most of the Sai devotees. *"Sai Rahem Nazar Karna"* and *"Raham Nazar Karo Ab More Sai"* or *"Aarti Sai Baba"* are usually sung.

Children should be encouraged to do *pranam* to Baba and explained about the basics of a puja. On holidays, the family can visit Baba's temple, or any temple in which Baba's statue is being worshipped. You can play Sai Aarti CD at home during puja. On holidays, you can offer cooked vegetarian food to Baba at home.

You can play the bhajan and aarti CDs in the car. Please go through the websites on Baba. Many of the sites contain Puja Vidhi and give a lot of information on Baba.

In all these situations, the devotee should always adjust with the prevailing situation and the prevailing rules of the country where he lives.

Q. **I have a small idol of Baba at home and a travelling job. How should I take care of Baba when I am travelling?**

A. There is a possibility that the entire family living in a foreign country might go out of home during holidays after locking up their house. Similarly, a person staying alone, when travelling out of town for work, may not be able to worship Baba daily at home.

I suggest that you can keep a small box made of wood, plastic, or metal, in which a small statue of Baba or a photo can be kept. Minimum puja items like smokeless candle, sandal powder, lighter, dry fruits, can also be kept inside this box. This small puja kit can be carried in the car or as a hand baggage (without the lighter, if you are flying) when leaving home for a different location. The puja can be done wherever you are.

Q. At times, we find news reports about the physical appearance of Baba at different places in India. Is it true? If so, when will Baba appear physically in Plano (Texas), US, where I stay?

A. I have been associated with the Sai movement for the last twenty-five years. I have the experience of being associated with the creation and running of hundreds of Sai temples, not only in India, but across the globe. However, I have never experienced such miracles in any of these temples or in the house of any of the devotees.

I don't believe in such sensational reports. It is better to worship Baba in a simple manner and serve the poor people in His name, rather than dabble in rumour mongering about miracles. A true devotee of Baba will not tell lies about the greatness of the Master by concocting stories.

Q. After building a temple of Baba in the USA, we feel frustrated because we don't progress further. How can we make progress in our activities relating to Shri Sai?

A. From my experience, I can say that it is easier to build a temple than to run it, be it in India or in the US. It is a little easier to run a temple in India because worship in most of the temples is done on a regular basis. The statues, photographs, pictures, and other items required for the puja, and also the reading material on Baba are available everywhere in India in plenty. Most of the towns and cities have Sai Baba temples. Many temples have come up in the rural areas as well. Further, it is much easier to get trained priests in India.

All these facilities are not so readily available in any other country. All these items and the priest will have to be brought from India to run the temple. The scarcity of priests is one of the major problems in foreign countries, particularly in the US because only a very small number of priests agree to go abroad, even if you can arrange a visa for them. When the priest goes back to India on leave or vacation, or is indisposed and unable to perform the puja and aarti, it becomes a difficult task to continue with the regular puja. It is, therefore, necessary that some of the devotees of Baba learn the Puja Vidhi and aarti. Thus, they can continue with the puja even in the absence of the priest. However, if possible, it is better to deploy a priest from another Hindu temple located in the area.

Plenty of CDs on *Baba's Aarti, Sai Mantras,* and the *Puja Vidhi* are available on the internet. If not, you can import these items from India. You can run the temples effectively in these countries only when dedicated groups of Sai devotees help one another to run them. You will benefit by communicating with other Sai devotees about the problems you face and try to get help from them. I have seen many temples in the US, Australia, Canada, and other countries running well in this manner.

Q. **When I become unsure of a certain situation, I always seek the help of Baba through Shri Sai Satcharita. I close my eyes, think of Baba, open *Satcharitra* at random, and try to interpret the writings in the opened page. Whatever is written there, I take it as the answer. Is this a correct thing to do?**

A. Before Shri Shirdi Sai Baba left His mortal body, devotees used to seek help directly from Him and get replies to their queries without any delay as they could meet Baba easily. After Baba left His mortal body, some devotees started the practice of opening Shri Sai Satcharita randomly and finding answers to their queries from the pages so opened. Such a tradition of seeking answers from Baba is continued by many of the devotees ever today.

It is reported that, for a devotee with a strong faith in Shri Shirdi Sai Baba, Shri Sai Satcharita provides replies to his queries, in whatever manner asked, and gives the correct answer. The assurances of Baba that He is always with His devotees seems to have been true in many cases, thus producing unwavering faith in Him.

Q. **When an issue makes me very restless and miserable, I usually look at Baba and place chits in front of Him. I pick up one of the chits with closed eyes and go by the decision of the chit. Am I doing the right thing?**

A. The practice of putting chits before a statue or picture of Baba to decide on certain issues in life has been an old practice with Sai devotees since the time of Baba. Many ardent and educated devotees of Baba like Kaka Saheb Dixit used to place chits before Baba's statue and pick up one of them to decide on major issues in life. Even today, thousands of devotees in India take recourse to this method when in distress.

In the ultimate analysis, the efficacy of this system depends on the strength of faith that a person reposes in Baba. Many devotees are said to have been benefited by making use of this chit system.

Q. **Is Shirdi Sai Baba movement outside India limited to the Indian diaspora?**

A. More and more devotees of different nationalities and origins, belonging to countries like US, Germany, and UK, have started following Shri Shirdi Sai Baba. With a lot of information on Him readily available, from the local communities around Baba's temples and also from the internet, this trend is bound to increase manifold in times to come.

Publication of articles related to Shri Shirdi Sai Baba, and His movement in periodicals like *Nova Religio* from the University of California Press at Berkeley, California, USA, and similar magazines in other countries, gives access to information on Baba to people of non-Indian descent. Besides, there exist many websites dedicated to Baba. Magazines and journals dealing exclusively with Shri Sai Movement in various Indian languages and English are available. In a few temples, foreigners are associated with the Sai movement.

It is interesting to know that many authors, who are not of Indian origin, have written excellent books on Baba. Some of them are: *Gurus Rediscovered: Biographies of Sai Baba and Upasani Maharaj of Sakori* by Kevin R.D. Shepherd, *The life and Teachings of Shirdi Sai Baba* by Antonio Rigopoulos, *Unraveling the Enigma (Shirdi Sai Baba in the Light of Sufism)* by Arthur Osborne, *The Incredible Sai Baba (The Life and Miracles of a Modern-Day Saint)* by Marianne Warren, *Sai Baba of Shirdi* by Perin S. Bharucha, etc.

Q. Are there any temples of Shirdi Sai Baba outside India? Where are they located?

A. It is reported that fully fledged Shirdi Sai Baba temples are located in United States of America, Canada, United Kingdom, Australia, New Zealand, Kenya, South Africa, and many other countries. It is also reported that prayer centres in some form or groups that meet regularly for performing bhajans, aartis of Baba, etc., exist in over 130 countries. Additionally, Baba's idol can be found in various Hindu temples along with other Deities. This has become the latest trend. As the number of Indians going abroad on jobs is increasing, so also are the Sai Baba temples.

There are a large number of Shirdi Sai Baba temples in many parts of the world. It would not be possible to produce a comprehensive list. However, names of some of the places where Shri Shirdi Sai Baba temples are located are mentioned here.

In USA, Sai temples are located at places like **Chicago**; **Illinois**—Shri Sai Baba Sansthan, 12N950 IL; Route 47, Hampshire, IL 60140; **Texas**—Houston; **Minnesota**—1835, Polk St, NE, Minneapolis, MN

55418; **Los Angeles; New York; Florida**—Shirdi Sai Baba Temple, 4707, Pleasant Grove Road, Inverness, Dist. Florida, Florida, etc. In **Australia**, Sai temples are located at **Melbourne, Sydney,** etc. In **Canada**, Shri Sai related activities are going on in **Toronto** and **Vancouver. Fiji** also has a Sai temple. In **UK**, the Sai temple is located at **Wembley, London,** etc. In **New Zealand**, Sai temples are located at **Auckland**—12–18 Princess St. Onehunga, Auckland and Shri Shirdi Sai Baba Sansthan of New Zealand Inc., P.O Box-16142, Sandringham, Auckland, etc. In **Malaysia**, Sai temples are located at **Kuala Lumpur,** etc. In **Hong Kong**, a Sai Baba temple is located at **Kowloon**.

You can find out details about these and other temples on the internet. It is reported that besides these, many more temples are coming up in countries like Sri Lanka, Japan, Germany, and in many countries in Europe.

Q. **I have come across the website saibaba.org and found your name there. Are you associated with it?**

A. Before the advent of internet, some devotees residing in Chicago started a bulletin board group which, subsequently in 1996, became the website saibaba.org. This group conducted *Sai Utsav*, the first international Sai conference in Chicago, in the year 2000, where I was invited to speak on Baba. This was followed by conferences in UK and Australia in 2001, and in Johannesburg and Nairobi in 2002. I had the good fortune to be with Sai devotees in these various countries and addressed them. The group also organized *Shirdi Sai Chitra Yatra* across United States and Canada in 2003. In 2004, saibaba.org inaugurated the Shirdi Sai temple in Hampshire, a suburb of Chicago. The website has been doing yeoman service to Sai devotees across the world and I have had the occasion to be a part of events related to Shri Shirdi Sai periodically.

Q. Is there any difference between the functioning of Shirdi Sai temples located in India and outside India? How and when should we visit Sai temples in countries like US and Canada?

A. The timings of opening and closing of temples varies from place to place. If someone is travelling and would like to visit a temple or a prayer centre in the US, Canada, Europe, Australia, or any other country, he is advised to first check the opening and closing timings from the organization running the temple.

In many temples, religious congregations take place mainly on Saturdays, Sundays, and other holidays. We must appreciate that the temples in the US and other countries have to and should follow the regulations of those countries. The devotees, as much as the Sai organizations, should adjust with such requirements. For example, unlike India, in the US most of the Sai devotees have to report for duty by 8:00 a.m. and work for eight hours up to 5:00 p.m., with a short lunch break. Usually, they travel long distances by car for their jobs and return home, sometimes as late as 8:00 p.m. or even later. Therefore, it may not be possible for them to visit temples in the morning or evening on a working day. They generally do so only during weekends, holidays, or vacations.

Holi, Dussehra, and Kali Puja are treated as holidays in most of the functional sectors in India — Government, corporate, or private. However, if these holidays happen to fall on weekdays, in the US and other countries, the devotees may not be able to visit the temples to celebrate these occasions. They usually celebrate such religious functions on the preceding or following Saturdays or Sundays.

Q. **How can a devotee outside India connect with activities of Shirdi Sai Baba spearheaded by you?**
A. Events related to Shri Shirdi Sai Baba are generally announced by the concerned trusts and organizations that organize them. Both pre and post event information is usually available on the internet, print, and social media sites. Additionally, many journals, periodicals, and e-magazines carry articles and information related to our activities. You can easily subscribe to any one of the above channels of communication to connect with the different Shirdi Sai activities happening around the world. For further information, you can connect by email at info@heritageofshirdisai.org or at the website saibaba.org.

Q. **My grandparents, who recently visited us from India, talk so much about Shirdi Sai Baba. How can I learn more about Him?**
A. The life and teachings of Shirdi Sai Baba are chronicled in the book Shri Sai Satcharita. This book was originally written in Marathi language in a verse form by Raghunath Dhabolkar also known as Hemadpant. It has been translated into English and almost all the regional languages of India. This is one of the most popular books that has been published by Shri Shirdi Sai Baba Sansthan and is made available to the devotees by the Sansthan.

There are many other books and periodicals about the Sai Movement from the time of Baba to the present day. Children may easily understand stories relating to Baba from books and periodicals specially written for them. Additionally, they may benefit immensely by participating in activities organized by temples of Shirdi Sai Baba or prayer centres. Please go through the available websites on Baba and you will get more information.

The online link of the Shirdi Sai Baba Sansthan is: www.shrisaibabasansthan.org

Q. I recently visited Shirdi Sai Baba temple in Chicago and found it very peaceful. I was raised as a Catholic. My mind is in conflict. Please advise me.

A. Shirdi Sai Baba never advocated nor advised anyone to change his religion or faith. The stories of His life show that He encouraged everyone to follow his own religion and beliefs. He focused more on bringing about fundamental changes that will lead a person towards a happy and pious life. The theme of His teachings rests on helping (serving) humanity, especially the downtrodden and underprivileged sections of the society, with love and compassion. A person can surely follow his own religion and be guided by the stories from Shri Shirdi Sai's life that appeal to him.

Humanism and not religion was the main theme of Baba. Baba was extremely compassionate towards the human beings who were discarded by the society. Similarly, Jesus Christ is one of the kindest souls that the world has witnessed.

Q. I live in Aberdeen, UK, where there is no temple of Baba. I want to be of service to Shri Shirdi Sai Baba. What can I do?

A. Shirdi Sai movement across the globe is being propelled by self-motivated devotees, who contribute their time and resources to propagate the Master's life and teachings. Service to the cause for which Shirdi Sai Baba stood is being carried out individually as well as collectively in groups by the Sai devotees.

At the individual level, you can start with the distribution of books like Shri Sai Satcharita and periodicals like *Sai Leela*, and *Heritage of Shirdi Sai* in English and in various Indian languages, within your known circle. You can hold prayer or bhajan and aarti singing gatherings at your home, just like the tradition of performing *Shri Satyanarayan Katha Vrat* on the prescribed dates. A group of devotees can conduct regular prayer meetings in their houses, turn by turn, on Thursdays. It is always convenient to perform the group pujas holding *Bhajan Sandhyas* on Saturdays, Sundays, or other holidays.

The group of devotees can further evolve into a Shirdi Sai congregation with full-fledged prayer services in a temple or a community centre. Keeping in constant touch with other groups and organizations will expand the movement.

Q. **I have just arrived in Australia as a student and am looking for the book Shri Sai Satcharita. Where can I get it?**

A. Shri Sai Satcharita, the book written on the life and teachings of Shri Shirdi Sai Baba, is available both in the print and the electronic media. The original book was written in Marathi in verse form. The book is usually referred to as *Pothi*. A condensed version of this book is published in English, Telugu, Tamil, Kannada, Gujarati, Marathi, Sindhi, Urdu, and Hindi from Shri Shirdi Sai Baba Sansthan Trust, Shirdi.

You can get this book from the Shirdi Sai Baba Sansthan at a nominal cost. Most of the temples and prayer centres in India and abroad carry copies of the book for sale and distribution. Verse to verse translation in English and Hindi from the Marathi language is also available from Sterling Publishers Pvt. Ltd., New Delhi. In Odia language, it is published by Vision Publishers Pvt. Ltd., Bhubaneshwar. You can visit the website of Shirdi Sai Baba Trust for more information.

The web address of the Shirdi Sai Baba Sansthan is shrisaibabasansthan.org which has a link to Shri Sai Satcharita in 15 languages.

Q. **I attended a *Sai Bhajan Sandhya* at Houston and would also like to organize a similar event where I live. Can you please guide me?**

A. It is a noble act to organize an event of any size and any nature in the name of Shri Shirdi Sai Baba, the incarnation of the Age. Events like the one you mention help in propagating the life and teachings of the Master and help you to reach out to others in the community. Such events begin with an organizational plan, created by a core group of devotees who share similar views.

Outside India, it is more convenient for devotees to share and get together on the internet via social media or website. It is better that the core group members meet frequently in one another's house and discuss about Baba, read Shri Sai Satcharita, and worship Him.

Once the organizing group is in place, then you can benchmark the format used by others or create a unique format specific to your group. You can start with smaller groups, with small events like *Sai Satcharita Parayana* and grow as you gain experience. Regardless of the number of people participating, the goal is to achieve maximum good of a maximum number of people.

Q. **How can an ordinary or common person render service to Baba?**

A. A person who wants to render service to Baba needs to have a strong sense of commitment and faith in Him, as well as a lot of patience. If you live near a Baba's temple, then you can offer to work there as a volunteer and be of service to Baba.

Baba's basic theme is humanism and the universality of one sovereign God. Any act performed in the cause of humanity can be taken up as a service to Baba, especially when such service is rendered to the underprivileged and the downtrodden. Participating in major relief activities for the community in natural disasters is a noble act. You can get involved as much as you like in community service, depending on the time and resources you have. Further, you can help to propagate the teachings of Shirdi Sai within your social circle and use the internet as an effective tool for this purpose.

Q. What is the easiest way to follow the teachings of Shirdi Sai Baba? Please guide.

A. As explained in Shri Sai Satcharita, Baba once pointed out that the spiritual path He prescribes is difficult and full of hazards. Having said so, He continued to assure the devotees that if His life and teachings are followed with faith and patience, then He would certainly be with His devotees. Hence, it is imperative that the devotees begin to absorb the teachings of Baba by going through books and magazines and listening to or watching the information available in the print, audio, or video form. The primary book of significance for Sai devotees is Shri Sai Satcharita. A regular study of this book is suggested for all the devotees who are desirous of following the path of Shri Sai.

Q. Is the worship of a picture of Baba as good as the worship of His statue? Sorry to ask this question, Guruji, but this is because I don't have a statue of Baba.

A. Many stories are documented about the life of Shri Shirdi Sai Baba, which emphatically state that His picture is as divine as His physical presence or statue. Before Shama started his journey for Prayag, Baba had told him, "I will be there before you." This statement had baffled Shama. Yet, when he reached Prayag, he discovered that in the house where he was offered boarding, a big picture of Baba was present. What Shama felt and experienced then, is eloquently described in Shri Sai Satcharita.

In another incident, when a devotee reached Shirdi for the first time, Baba told him very lovingly, "We have met before." The devotee could not understand the meaning of Baba's comment and got confused. Suddenly, he recalled that he had bowed before a picture of Baba a few years prior to his trip.

And then again, Baba gave a dream to Hemadpant that He will join for dinner at his house. At the appropriate time of dinner, Baba came to his home in the form of a picture, carried by someone, and the entire family enjoyed their dinner after offering it to Baba.

Many more stories are available on this aspect of Baba. When a person approaches, prostrates, and prays in front of Baba's picture with the same devotional fervour as he would do if He were present, he will reap huge rewards.

Q. **I am a devotee of foreign origin. Can you please explain the gist of Shirdi Sai Baba's preachings?**

A. In its quintessence, the philosophy of Shri Shirdi Sai Baba stands for certain ideals. They are:

1. There always exists one and only one God, who is the Supreme and Sovereign Power, both spiritual and temporal, of the universe. Baba used to address this power as Ishwar or Allah.
2. All living beings, including human beings, are His subjects and He takes care of all of them. Everyone should render prayers to Him and surrender to Him.
3. All human beings are His children; there should be no differential treatment between individuals on the grounds of caste, creed, race, language, religion, sex or colour. The rich and poor, the happy and the unhappy, the healthy and the diseased, the ruler and the beggar, all should be treated with equal dignity, because all are the children of God.
4. Purity of mind and devotion towards the Guru and/or God is the cardinal requirement for the spiritual evolution of an individual.

5. It is impossible for an individual, however intelligent and hardworking, to realize God without the help of a Sadguru. The help, kindness, and complete support of a Guru is vitally and continuously required by a spiritual practitioner, till he himself becomes a Sadguru.
   I would suggest that you search for more information and details from the websites on internet. More than a thousand sites on Shri Shirdi Sai Baba are available.

Q. **I am staying at Dublin. I use Baba's Udi regularly. When the stock of Udi gets exhausted, how do I get it?**

A. You can get Udi through your friends and relatives who visit Shirdi. You can become an online member of Shri Sai Baba Sansthan, Shirdi, on payment of a small amount of money. Once you are a member, the Sansthan will regularly send you the Udi.

You can also get Udi by communicating with the concerned persons through the websites mentioned below:
www.saibaba.org
www.saidhamsola.org/freeprasad.php

Q. **My husband and I are extremely interested in seeing Baba's live aartis taking place in the Samadhi Mandir at Shirdi. Can you please suggest the way?**

A. Baba's live and recorded aartis can be found on many websites. Four aartis are performed daily at Shirdi Sai Baba Samadhi Mandir at Shirdi. The Shri Shirdi Sai Baba Sansthan has an official internet website shrisaibabasansthan.org which relays all the four aartis. Another Hindi channel called *Darshan* also relays the four aartis every day. The link for live darshan is: www.shrisaibabasansthan.org/darshanflash_1.html

Our Books on SHIRDI SAI BABA

Shirdi Sai Baba is a household name in India as well as in many parts of the World today. These books offer fascinating glimpses into the life and miracles of Shirdi Sai Baba and other Perfect Masters. These books will provide you with an experience that is bound to transform one's sense of perspective and bring about perceptible and meaningful spiritual growth.

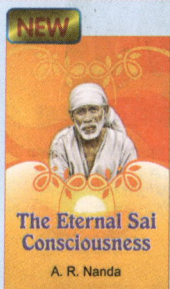

The Eternal Sai Consciousness
A. R. Nanda
ISBN 978 81 207 9043 8
₹ 200

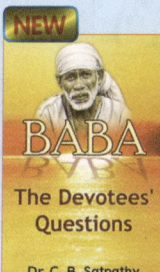

BABA:
The Devotees' Questions
Dr. C. B. Satpathy
ISBN 978 81 207 8966 1
₹ 150

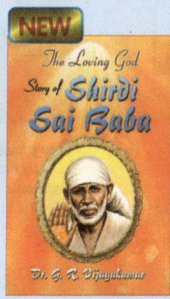

The Loving God:
Story of Shirdi Sai Baba
Dr. G. R. Vijayakumar
ISBN 978 81 207 8079 8
₹ 200

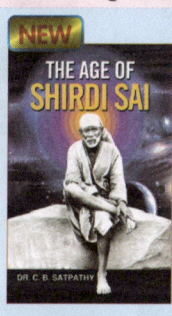

The Age of Shirdi Sai
Dr. C. B. Satpathy
ISBN 978 81 207 8700 1
₹ 225

Sai Samartha and Ramana Maharshi
S. Seshadri
ISBN 978 81 207 8986 9
₹150

Shri Sai Satcharita
The Life and Teachings of Shirdi Sai Baba
Translated by Indira Kher
ISBN 978 81 207 2211 8
₹ 500(HB)
ISBN 978 81 207 2153 1
₹ 300(PB)

Sree Sai Charitra Darshan
Mohan Jagannath Yadav
ISBN 978 81 207 8346 1
₹ 200

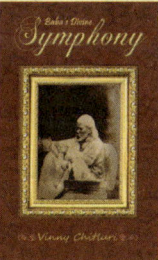

Baba's Divine Symphony
Vinny Chitluri
ISBN 978 81 207 8485 7
₹ 250

Sai Baba an Incarnation
Bela Sharma
ISBN 978 81 207 8833 6
₹ 200

Shirdi Sai Baba: The Perfect Master
Suresh Chandra Panda & Smita Panda
ISBN 978 81 207 8113 9
₹ 200

SHIRDI within & beyond
A collection of unseen & rare photographs
Dr. Rabinder Nath Kakarya
ISBN 978 81 207 7806 1
₹ 750

Shri Sai Baba
Teachings & Philosophy
Lt Col M B Nimbalkar
ISBN 978 81 207 2364 1
₹ 100

The Eternal Sai Phenomenon
A R Nanda
ISBN 978 81 207 6086 8
₹ 200

God Who Walked on Earth:
The Life & Times of Shirdi Sai Baba
Rangaswami Parthasarathy
ISBN 978 81 207 1809 8
₹ 150

STERLING

SHIRDI SAI BABA

Baba's Rinanubandh
Leelas during His Sojourn in Shirdi
Compiled by Vinny Chitluri
ISBN 978 81 207 3403 6
₹ 200

Baba's Gurukul
SHIRDI
Vinny Chitluri
ISBN 978 81 207 4770 8
₹ 200

Baba's Anurag
Love for His Devotees
Compiled by Vinny Chitluri
ISBN 978 81 207 5447 8
₹ 125

Baba's Vaani: His Sayings and Teachings
Compiled by Vinny Chitluri
ISBN 978 81 207 3859 1
₹ 200

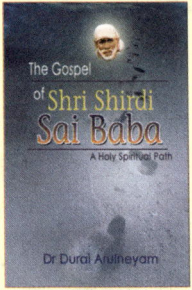

The Gospel of Shri Shirdi Sai Baba: A Holy Spiritual Path
Dr Durai Arulneyam
ISBN 978 81 207 3997 0
₹ 150

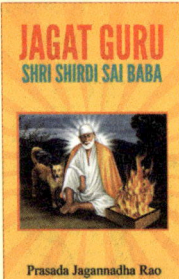

Jagat Guru: Shri Shirdi Sai Baba
Prasada Jagannadha Rao
ISBN 978 81 207 8175 7
₹ 100

Spotlight on the Sai Story
Chakor Ajgaonker
ISBN 978 81 207 4399 1
₹ 125

Shirdi Sai Baba A Practical God
K. K. Dixit
ISBN 978 81 207 5918 3
₹ 75

Life History of Shirdi Sai Baba
Ammula Sambasiva Rao
ISBN 978 81 207 7722 4
₹ 150

I am always with you
Lorraine Walshe-Ryan
ISBN 978 81 207 3192 9
₹ 150

BABA- May I Answer
C.B. Satpathy
ISBN 978 81 207 4594 0
₹ 150

Unravelling the Enigma: Shirdi Sai Baba in the light of Sufism
Marianne Warren
ISBN 978 81 207 2147 0
₹ 400

STERLING

Sab Ka Malik Ek

**Shirdi Sai Baba
The Divine Healer**
Raj Chopra
ISBN 978 81 207 4766 1
₹ 100

**Shirdi Sai Baba and
other Perfect Masters**
C B Satpathy
ISBN 978 81 207 2384 9
₹ 150

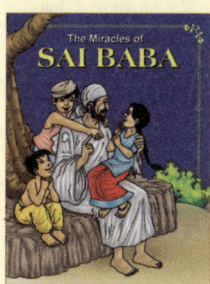

The Miracles of Sai Baba
ISBN 978 81 207 5433 1 (HB)
₹ 250

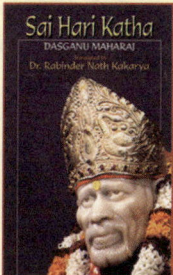

Sai Hari Katha
*Dasganu Maharaj Translated by
Dr. Rabinder Nath Kakarya*
ISBN 978 81 207 3324 4
₹ 100

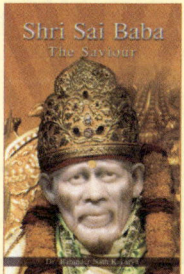

Shri Sai Baba- The Saviour
Dr. Rabinder Nath Kakarya
ISBN 978 81 207 4701 2
₹ 100

Sai Baba's 261 Leelas
Balkrishna Panday
ISBN 978 81 207 2727 4
₹ 125

Sri Sai Baba
*Sai Sharan Anand
Translated by V.B Kher*
ISBN 978 81 207 1950 7
₹ 200

Sai Baba: His Divine Glimpses
V B Kher
ISBN 978 81 207 2291 0
₹ 95

**Ek An English Musical on the
Life of Shirdi Sai Baba**
Usha Akella
ISBN 978 81 207 6842 0
₹ 75

**A Diamond Necklace To:
Shirdi Sai Baba**
Giridhar Ari
ISBN 978 81 207 5868 1
₹ 200

**A Solemn Pledge from
True Tales of
Shirdi Sai Baba**
Dr B H Briz-Kishore
ISBN 978 81 207 2240 8
₹ 95

**Shri Shirdi Sai Baba: His
Life and Miracles**
ISBN 978 81 207 2877 6
₹ 30

STERLING

SHIRDI SAI BABA

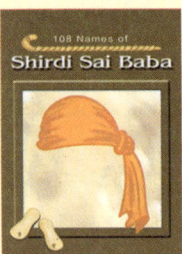

108 Names of Shirdi Sai Baba
ISBN 978 81 207 3074 8
₹ 50

Shirdi Sai Baba Aratis
ISBN 978 81 207 8456 7
(English)   ₹ 10

Shirdi Sai Speaks... Sab Ka Malik Ek
Quotes for the Day
ISBN 978 81 207 3101 1
₹ 200

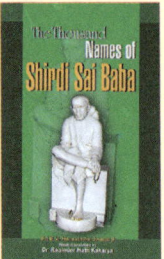

The Thousand Names of Shirdi Sai Baba
Sri B.V. Narasimha Swami Ji
Hindi translation by
Dr. Rabinder Nath Kakarya
ISBN 978 81 207 3738 9
₹ 75

Shirdi Sai Baba Box

Shri Sai Baba
978 81 207 6920 5
Box size: 23.5 x 16.5 cm
₹ 900

Shri Sai Satcharitra

Sai Baba Mandiramdhil Arataya & Mantrochar - Mp3

Vibhuti

Sai Baba Photo Frame

Dateless Calendar

Lord Sri Dattatreya The Trinity
Dwarika Mohan Mishra
ISBN 978 81 207 5417 1
₹ 200

Divine Gurus

Guru Charitra
Shree Swami Samarth
ISBN 978 81 207 3348 0
₹ 200

Sri Swami Samarth Maharaj of Akkalkot
N.S. Karandikar
ISBN 978 81 207 3445 6
₹ 200

Hazrat Babajan:
A Pathan Sufi of Poona
Kevin R. D. Shepherd
ISBN 978 81 207 8698 1
₹ 200

Sri Narasimha Swami Apostle of Shirdi Sai Baba
Dr. G.R. Vijayakumar
ISBN 978 81 207 4432 5
₹ 90

STERLING

श्री शिरडी साई बाबा

जेल में साई साक्षात्कार
राकेश जुनेजा
978 81 207 9063 6
₹ 150

श्री साई चरित्र दर्शन
मोहन जगन्नाथ यादव
978 81 207 8350 8
₹ 200

श्री साई सच्चरित्र
श्री शिरडी साई बाबा की अद्भुत
जीवनी तथा उनके अमूल्य उपदेश
गोविंद रघुनाथ दाभोलकर (हेमाडपंत)
978 81 207 2501 0   ₹ 250 (PB)
978 81 207 2500 3   ₹ 300 (HB)

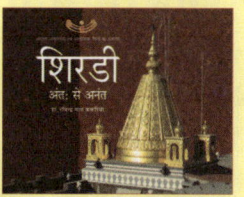
शिरडी अंतः से अनंत
डॉ. रबिन्द्रनाथ ककरिया
978 81 207 8191 7
₹ 750

साई सुमिरन
अंजु टंडन
978 81 207 8706 3
₹ 90

बाबा की वाणी-उनके
वचन तथा आदेश
बेला शर्मा
978 81 207 4745 6
₹ 100

बाबा का अनुराग
विनी चितलुरी
978 81 207 6699 0
₹ 100

बाबा का ऋणानुबंध
विनी चितलुरी
978 81 207 5998 5
₹ 150

बाबा का गुरुकुल-शिरडी
विनी चितलुरी
978 81 207 6698 3
₹ 125

साई की आत्मकथा
विकास कपूर
978 81 207 7719 4
₹ 200

बाबा-आध्यात्मिक विचार
चन्द्रभानु सतपथी
978 81 207 4627 5
₹ 150

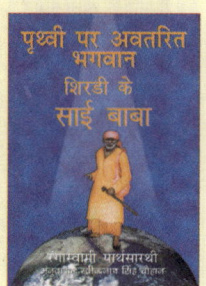
पृथ्वी पर अवतरित
भगवान शिरडी के साई बाबा
रंगास्वामी पार्थसारथी
978 81 207 2101 2
₹ 150

स्टर्लिंग

श्री शिरडी साई बाबा

श्री शिरडी साई बाबा एवं अन्य सद्‌गुरु
चन्द्रभानु सतपथी
978 81 207 4401 1
₹ 90

साई शरण में
चन्दुभानु सतपथी
978 81 207 2802 8
₹ 150

साई – सबका मालिक
कल्पना भाकुनी
978 81 207 3320 6
₹ 125

साई बाबा एक अवतार
बेला शर्मा
978 81 207 6706 5
₹ 100

साई सत्‌ चरित का प्रकाश
बेला शर्मा
978 81 207 7804 7
₹ 200

श्री साई बाबा के परम भक्त
डॉ. रबिन्द्रनाथ ककरिया
978 81 207 2779 3
₹ 75

श्री साई बाबा के उपदेश व तत्त्वज्ञान
लेफ्टिनेन्ट कर्नल
एम. बी. निंबालकर
978 81 207 5971 8   ₹ 100

साई भक्तानुभव
डॉ. रबिन्द्रनाथ ककरिया
978 81 207 3052 6
₹ 125

श्री साई बाबा के अनन्य भक्त
डॉ. रबिन्द्र नाथ ककरिया
978 81 207 2705 2
₹ 100

साई का संदेश
डॉ. रबिन्द्र नाथ ककरिया
978 81 207 2879 0
₹ 125

शिरडी सम्पूर्ण दर्शन
डॉ. रबिन्द्रनाथ ककरिया
978 81 207 2312 2
₹ 50

मुक्तिदाता – श्री साई बाबा
डॉ. रबिन्द्रनाथ ककरिया
978 81 207 2778 6
₹ 65